G000153720

Easy PC Keyboard Shortcuts

Books Available

By the same authors:

BP548 Easy PC Keyboard Shortcuts*
BP546 Microsoft Works Suite 2004 explained
BP545 Paint Shop Pro 8 explained*
BP544 Microsoft Office 2003 explained
BP538 Windows XP for beginners*
BP525 Controlling Windows XP the easy way*
BP522 Microsoft Works Suite 2002 explained
BP514 Windows XP explained*
BP513 Internet Explorer 6 and Outlook Express 6 explained*
BP512 Microsoft Access 2002 explained
BP511 Microsoft Excel 2002 explained
BP510 Microsoft Word 2002 explained
BP509 Microsoft Office XP explained
BP505 Microsoft Works Suite 2001 explained
BP498 Using Visual Basic
BP493 Windows Me explained*
BP491 Windows 2000 explained*
BP487 Quicken 2000 UK explained*
BP486 Using Linux the easy way*
BP465 Lotus SmartSuite Millennium explained
BP456 Windows 98 explained*
BP448 Lotus SmartSuite 97 explained
BP433 Your own Web site on the Internet
BP341 MS-DOS explained
BP284 Programming in QuickBASIC
BP258 Learning to Program in C

If you would like to purchase a Companion Disc for any of the listed books by the same authors, apart from the ones marked with an asterisk, containing the file/program listings which appear in them, then fill in the form at the back of the book and send it to Phil Oliver at the stipulated address.

Easy PC Keyboard Shortcuts

by

P.R.M. Oliver
and
N. Kantaris

Bernard Babani (publishing) Ltd
The Grampians
Shepherds Bush Road
London W6 7NF
England
www.babanibooks.com

Please Note

Although every care has been taken with the production of this book to ensure that any projects, designs, modifications and/or programs, etc., contained herewith, operate in a correct and safe manner and also that any components specified are normally available in Great Britain, the Publishers and Author(s) do not accept responsibility in any way for the failure (including fault in design) of any project, design, modification or program to work correctly or to cause damage to any equipment that it may be connected to or used in conjunction with, or in respect of any other damage or injury that may be so caused, nor do the Publishers accept responsibility in any way for the failure to obtain specified components.

Notice is also given that if equipment that is still under warranty is modified in any way or used or connected with home-built equipment then that warranty may be void.

© 2004 BERNARD BABANI (publishing) LTD

First Published - August 2004

British Library Cataloguing in Publication Data:

A catalogue record for this book is available from the British Library

ISBN 0 85934 548 3

Cover Design by Gregor Arthur
Printed and Bound in Great Britain by Cox & Wyman Ltd, Reading

About this Book

Many actions carried out on a PC have keyboard shortcuts attached to them. These are especially useful for people who are more used to the keyboard than to a mouse. For touch typists they are essential. But anyone who takes the trouble to learn these shortcuts will find they can work far faster and more efficiently than using just menu systems or toolbar buttons.

The book describes the keyboard shortcuts for:

- Microsoft Windows XP and its accessories
- Windows Media Player 9
- Internet Explorer 6
- Outlook 2003 and Outlook Express 6
- Microsoft Office 2003
- Word XP and 2003
- Excel 2003
- Access 2003
- Publisher 2003
- Powerpoint 2003
- Frontpage 2003
- Microsoft Works Suite 2004 and Works 7.0
- Paint Shop Pro 8
- Adobe Reader 6
- Adobe Acrobat 6

Although the shortcuts listed are for the latest versions of these programs when we went to print, many will work with older programs. With a little trial and error, the book will be useful to anyone using almost any versions of the above software.

This book *Easy PC Keyboard Shortcuts* was written using a PC running under Windows XP. It is meant for any PC user, from beginners to 'power users'. We do not suggest that you sit down and read the book from cover to cover, just dip in wherever you want. Each chapter covers the shortcuts of a particular application. When you are using that application it makes a very useful desktop companion.

When you are looking for a particular shortcut, we suggest you first explore the Contents pages at the end of this chapter. Then try the index. We have tried to make this as useful as possible.

The book doesn't describe the actual workings of the application programs covered, or of Microsoft Windows, or how to set up your computer hardware. If you need to know more about any of these, then may we suggest that you refer to our other books, also published by BERNARD BABANI (publishing) Ltd, and listed on page ii earlier in this book.

All in all we included the material that we often have to search around for ourselves! Good luck with the book and we hope you enjoy using it and that it helps to speed up your PC work.

About the Authors

Phil Oliver graduated in Mining Engineering at Camborne School of Mines and has specialised in most aspects of surface mining technology, with a particular emphasis on computer related techniques. He has worked in Guyana, Canada, several Middle Eastern and Central Asian countries, South Africa and the United Kingdom, on such diverse projects as: the planning and management of bauxite, iron, gold and coal mines; rock excavation contracting in the UK; international mining equipment sales and international mine consulting. He later took up a lecturing position at Camborne School of Mines (part of Exeter University) in Surface Mining and Management. He has now retired, to spend more time writing, consulting, and developing Web sites.

Noel Kantaris graduated in Electrical Engineering at Bristol University and after spending three years in the Electronics Industry in London, took up a Tutorship in Physics at the University of Queensland. Research interests in Ionospheric Physics, led to the degrees of M.E. in Electronics and Ph.D. in Physics. On return to the UK, he took up a Post-Doctoral Research Fellowship in Radio Physics at the University of Leicester, and then a lecturing position in Engineering at the Camborne School of Mines, Cornwall, (part of Exeter University), where he was also the CSM Computing Manager. At present he is IT Director of FFC Ltd.

Acknowledgements

We would like to thank all of our friends and colleagues, for their helpful tips and suggestions which assisted us in the writing of this book.

Trademarks

Arial and **Times New Roman** are registered trademarks of The Monotype Corporation plc.

HP and LaserJet are registered trademarks of Hewlett Packard Corporation.

Microsoft, **MS-DOS** and **Windows**, are either registered trademarks or trademarks of Microsoft Corporation.

Paint Shop, **Paint Shop Pro** and **Jasc** are either registered trademarks or trademarks of Jasc Software Inc.

Adobe, Acrobat, Reader and **PostScript** are registered trademarks, or trademarks, of Adobe Systems Incorporated.

All other brand and product names used in the book are recognised as trademarks, or registered trademarks, of their respective companies.

Contents

1

Getting Started

When we first started using computers, graphic interfaces like Windows and pointing tools like mice, had not been invented. The keyboard had to be used for everything, for entering data as well as the commands to manipulate it. Like most people in those days we became quite proficient with the keyboard. Times have changed. As Windows has improved as an operating system, pretty well all modern software is designed to be used graphically. You can now spend over half your time using a mouse to move you around a document and to find your way through menus and deep layers of dialogue boxes.

But if you watch a 'professional typist' he, or she, will still use the keyboard for most of the time. The majority of the programs regularly used today are built with a range of keyboard shortcuts. Touch typists find it much easier to learn and use these instead of taking their hands off the keyboard to pick up and play with a mouse.

You too can save time and effort and boost your productivity by spending some time in the following chapters. We explain the hundreds of keyboard shortcuts built into Windows XP the Microsoft Office applications, and some other favourite applications. Some of these are very well known, but some very useful shortcuts never seem to have been brought out into the open air.

This how-to reference guide will provide you with the information to save you time, simplify your keystrokes, and probably more important in the long run, reduce mouse stress to your wrists, arms and shoulders.

Keyboard Shortcuts

A keyboard shortcut is a function key, such as **F5**, or a key combination, such as **Ctrl+A**, that you use to carry out a menu command, or open a tool. An access key, on the other hand, is a key combination, such as **Alt+F**, that moves the focus to a menu, command, or control.

Using Access Keys in Menu Bars

In most Windows applications you can carry out menu bar operations using just keystrokes. Each menu bar option has associated with it a pull-down sub-menu. To activate the menu, press the **Alt** key, which causes the first option of the menu to be selected, then use the right and left arrow keys to highlight any of the options in the menu. Pressing the **Enter** key, reveals the pull-down sub-menu of the highlighted menu option. The sub-menu of Microsoft Word's **File** option is shown here.

Menu options can also be activated directly by pressing the **Alt** key followed by the underlined letter of the required option. Thus, pressing **Alt+F**, opens the pull-down **File** sub-menu. You can use the up and down arrow keys to move the highlighted bar up and down a sub-menu, or the right and left arrow keys to move along the options in the menu bar. Pressing the **Enter** key selects the highlighted option or executes the highlighted command. Pressing the **Esc** key once, closes the pull-down sub-menu, while pressing the **Esc** key for a second time, closes the menu system.

2

Microsoft Windows XP

Windows XP at the time of writing is Microsoft's latest desktop Operating System (OS). It comes in two versions, a Professional or a Home edition. The keyboard shortcuts are the same for both versions.

About Windows XP

Windows XP is a 32-bit Operating System which, just like its predecessors (Windows 95/98/Me/2000), uses a Graphical Interface.

It is an easier to run and more efficient operating system to install, far more stable, and for business users the Professional edition is less expensive to deploy for a large number of networked computers. Microsoft has employed the scripting process, first encountered in Windows 2000, which automates the installation process and makes it a lot easier, particularly for large networks. Ordinary desktop users also benefit as this version of Windows is by far the easiest to install and the most stable to operate under.

Keyboard Shortcuts

The following is a list of Windows XP keyboard shortcuts. You can use them as an alternative to the mouse when working in Windows. You can open, close, and navigate the *start* menu, desktop, menus, dialogue boxes, and Web pages using these shortcuts.

Some keyboard shortcuts may not work if 'StickyKeys' is turned on in the Accessibility Options.

Common to Most Windows Programs

These shortcuts can be used in almost all Windows based programs. The editing shortcuts are the most useful to remember of all, as they can be used to copy and paste selected (highlighted) text to anywhere you can enter it. For example, you can 'pick up' a long Web address from an e-mail or Web page with the **Ctrl+C** shortcut, and paste it into any text box using **Ctrl+V**. This is easier than remembering, or writing down the text, and makes errors far less likely.

Ctrl+X	Cut.
Ctrl+C	Copy.
Ctrl+V	Paste.
Ctrl+Z	Undo.
Delete	Delete.
Ctrl+B	Bold.
Ctrl+U	Underline.
Ctrl+I	Italic.

General Keyboard Shortcuts

F1	Open the Help system.
F2	Rename selected item.
Ctrl+Esc	Display the *start* menu.
Alt+F4	Close the active item, or exit the active program.

Alt+Tab	Switch between open programs.
Shift+Delete	Delete selected item permanently without placing the item in the Recycle Bin.
Ctrl+A	Select all.
F3	Search for a file or folder.
Alt+Enter	View properties for the selected item.
Alt+Space	Open the shortcut menu for the active window.
Ctrl+F4	Close the active document in programs that allow you to have multiple documents open simultaneously.
Alt+Esc	Cycle through programs in the order they were opened.
F6	Cycle through screen elements in a window, or on the desktop.
F4	Display the Address bar list in My Computer or Windows Explorer.
Shift+F10	Display the shortcut menu for the selected item.
Alt+Space	Display the System menu for the active window.
F10	Activate the menu bar in the active program.
⇨	Open the next menu to the right, or open a sub-menu.
⇦	Open the next menu to the left, or close a sub-menu.
F5	Refresh the active window.
Backspace	View the folder one level up in My Computer or Windows Explorer.
Esc	Cancel the current task.
Shift	When you insert a CD into the CD-ROM drive prevents the CD from automatically playing.
Ctrl+⇨	Move the insertion point to the beginning of the next word.

Ctrl+ ⇐	Move the insertion point to the beginning of the previous word.
Ctrl+ ⇓	Move the insertion point to the beginning of the next paragraph.
Ctrl+ ⇑	Move the insertion point to the beginning of the previous paragraph.
Ctrl+Shift+Arrow	Highlight a block of text.
Shift+Arrow	Select more than one item in a window or on the desktop, or select text within a document.

Dialogue Box Shortcuts

Ctrl+Tab	Move forward through tabs.
Ctrl+Shift+Tab	Move backward through tabs.
Tab	Move forward through options.
Shift+Tab	Move backward through options.
Alt+Underline	Carry out the corresponding command or select the corresponding option.
Enter	Carry out the command for the active option or button.
Space	Select or clear the check box if the active option is a check box.
Arrow keys	Select a button if the active option is a group of option buttons.
F1	Display Help.
F4	Display the items in the active list.
Backspace	Open a folder one level up if a folder is selected in the Save As or Open dialogue box.

Natural Keyboard Shortcuts

You can use the following shortcuts with a Microsoft Natural Keyboard (or a compatible keyboard) that includes the Windows logo key ⊞ and the Application key ▤.

⊞	Display or hide the Start menu.
⊞+Break	Display the System Properties dialogue box.
⊞+D	Show the desktop.
⊞+M	Minimise all windows.
⊞+Shift+M	Restores minimised windows.
⊞+Tab	Successively highlights the running application icons on the Task bar. You then press **Enter** to open the application.
⊞+E	Open My Computer.
⊞+F	Search for a file or folder.
Ctrl+⊞+F	Search for computers.
⊞+F1	Display Windows Help.
⊞+ L	Lock your computer if you are connected to a network domain, or switch users if you are not connected to a network domain.
⊞+R	Open the Run dialogue box.
▤	Display the shortcut menu for the selected item.
⊞+U	Open Utility Manager.

Windows Explorer Shortcuts

Windows Explorer displays the hierarchical structure of files, folders, and drives on your computer, and lets you easily copy, move, rename, and search for files and folders. Once it is open you can use the following shortcuts.

Note - The **Num Lock** shortcuts use numeric keypad keys only.

End	Display the bottom of the active window.
Home	Display the top of the active window.
Num Lock+*	Display all sub-folders under the selected folder.
Num Lock+Plus	Display the contents of the selected folder.
Num Lock+Minus	Collapse the selected folder.
⇐	Collapse current selection if expanded, or select parent folder.
⇒	Display current selection if collapsed, or select first sub-folder.

Windows XP Tools and Accessories

The remainder of this chapter lists the keyboard shortcuts for the main tools and accessories that are installed with Windows XP.

The Windows Media Player shortcuts are presented on their own in the next chapter.

The Calculator

You can use the Calculator in Standard view to do simple calculations, or in Scientific view to do advanced scientific and statistical calculations. The following is an alphabetical list of Calculator buttons and their keyboard equivalents.

Button	Key	Button	Key
%	%	Hyp	h
(	(	Int	;
)	)	Inv	i
*	*	ln	n
+	+	log	l
+/-	F9	Lsh	<
-	-	M+	Ctrl+P
.	. or ,	MC	Ctrl+L
/	/	Mod	%
0-9	0-9	MR	Ctrl+R
1/x	r	MS	Ctrl+M
=	Enter	n!	!
A-F	A-F	Not	~
And	&	Oct	F7
Ave	Ctrl+A	Or	|(pipe)
Backspace	Backspace	pi	p
Bin	F8	Qword	F12
Byte	F4	Radians	F3
C	Esc	s	Ctrl+D
CE	Del	sin	s
cos	o	sqrt	@
Dat	Ins	Sta	Ctrl+S
Dec	F6	Sum	Ctrl+T
Degrees	F2	tan	t
dms	m	Word	F3
Dword	F2	Xor	^
Exp	x	x^2	@
F-E	v	x^3	#
Grads	F4	x^y	y
Hex	F5		

Character Map

You can use Character Map to copy and paste special characters into your documents, such as the trademark symbol, special mathematical characters, or a character from the character set of another language.

Once you double-click a character on the grid of characters in the Character Map, you can move through the grid using the following keyboard shortcuts:

⇒	Moves to the right or to the beginning of the next line.
⇐	Moves to the left or to the end of the previous line.
⇧	Moves up one row.
⇩	Moves down one row.
Page Up	Moves up one screen at a time.
Page Down	Moves down one screen at a time.
Home	Moves to the beginning of the line.
End	Moves to the end of the line.
Ctrl+Home	Moves to the first character.
Ctrl+End	Moves to the last character.
Space	Switches between enlarged and normal mode when a character is selected.

Notepad

Notepad is a basic text editor you can use to create and edit simple text files, with the **.txt** file type.

Ctrl+N	Create a new text file.
Ctrl+O	Open an existing text file.
Ctrl+S	Save the current file with the same name.
Ctrl+P	Open the Print dialogue box.
Ctrl+X	Cut selection to the clipboard.
Ctrl+C	Copy selection to the clipboard.
Ctrl+V	Paste clipboard contents.
Ctrl+A	Select all of the current page.
Del	Delete selected text.
Ctrl+F	Start a search operation.
F3	Next search result.
Ctrl+H	Start a search and replace operation.
Ctrl+G	Go to.
F5	Place a time and date stamp.

WordPad

You can use WordPad to create or edit large text files that can contain formatting or graphics.

Ctrl+N	Create a new text file.
Ctrl+O	Open an existing text file.
Ctrl+S	Save the current file with the same name.
Ctrl+P	Open the Print dialogue box.
Ctrl+X	Cut selection to the clipboard.
Ctrl+C	Copy selection to the clipboard.
Ctrl+V	Paste clipboard contents.
Ctrl+Z	Undo the last action.
Ctrl+A	Select all of the current page.
Del	Clear selected text.
Ctrl+F	Start a search operation.
F3	Next search result.
Ctrl+H	Start a search and replace operation.
Alt+Enter	Edit an object's properties.

Microsoft Paint

Paint is a drawing tool you can use to create black-and-white or colour drawings that you can save as bitmap (.bmp) files. You can also use Paint to send your drawing in an e-mail, set the image as a desktop background, and save image files using different file formats.

Ctrl+N	Create a new drawing.
Ctrl+O	Open an existing drawing file.
Ctrl+S	Save the current file with the same name.
Ctrl+P	Open the Print dialogue box.
Alt+F4	Exit the Paint program.
Ctrl+X	Cut selection to the clipboard.
Ctrl+C	Copy selection to the clipboard.
Ctrl+V	Paste clipboard contents.
Ctrl+Z	Undo the last action.
Ctrl+Y	Repeat the last action.
Ctrl+A	Select all of the current drawing.
Del	Clear selection.
Ctrl+T	View/Hide the Toolbox.
Ctrl+L	View/Hide the Color box.
Ctrl+F	View the bitmap image full screen.
Ctrl+Page Down	Zoom to large size.
Ctrl+Page Up	Zoom down to normal size.
Ctrl+G	Show grid of pixels.
Ctrl+R	Flip or rotate the image.
Ctrl+W	Stretch or skew the image.
Ctrl+I	Invert the image colours.
Ctrl+E	Open the image attributes box.
Ctrl+Shift+N	Clear the image.

Windows Movie Maker

With Windows Movie Maker, you can transfer recorded video and audio from a source, such as an analogue camcorder or digital video camera, to your computer. In addition to using your own recorded content, you can also import existing audio and video files to use in the movies you create.

Ctrl+N	Create a new project.
Ctrl+O	Open an existing project.
Ctrl+S	Save a project with the same name.
F12	Save a project with a new name.
Ctrl+I	Import a file.
Ctrl+R	Start recording audio or movies.
Ctrl+X	Cut selection to the clipboard.
Ctrl+C	Copy selection to the clipboard.
Ctrl+V	Paste clipboard contents.
Ctrl+A	Select all.
Del	Delete selection.
F2	Rename project.
Ctrl+Shift+ ⇐	Set movie clip start trim point.
Ctrl+Shift+ ⇒	Set movie clip end trim point.
Ctrl+Shift+Del	Clear trim points.
Ctrl+Shift+S	Split movie clip.
Ctrl+Shift+C	Combine movie clips.
Space	Start/pause playing movie.
. (full stop)	Stop playing movie.
Alt + ⇐	Move to previous frame.
Alt + ⇒	Move to next frame.
Ctrl+Alt+ ⇐	Play backwards.
Ctrl+Alt+ ⇒	Play forwards.
Alt+Enter	View full screen.
F1	Open Movie Maker Help window.

3

Windows Media Player 9

Windows XP has many features built into it, one of which is the Media Player. This gives your PC the ability to handle multimedia, which put simply means it can play sound and moving image files.

About Windows Media Player

You can use Microsoft's Windows Media Player to play and organise digital media files on your computer and on the Internet.

You can use the Player to listen to radio stations from all over the world, play and copy CDs, create your own CDs, play DVDs, and copy music and videos to portable devices, such as portable digital audio players and Pocket PCs.

To play DVDs, you obviously need a DVD-ROM drive, but you also need a software or hardware DVD decoder installed on your computer. New PCs usually come with DVD decoder program already installed. If not, you should check the package, as a CD with the software on will probably be included amongst the many discs, etc., that come with it. You then need to install the software.

To make sure you have the latest version of the Media Player, log onto the Internet and use the **Help**, **Check For Player Updates** command from the Media Player main menu. We cover version 9 here.

Keyboard Shortcuts

All of Windows Media Player's features and buttons are accessible from the keyboard.

Commands, Buttons, and Menus.

ALT+V, G	Opens a menu to access the Now Playing, Media Guide, Copy from CD, Media Library, Radio Tuner, Copy to CD or Device, Premium Services, and Skin Chooser taskbar features.
Arrow keys	Move left and right or up and down on menus or lists.
	You can also use the arrow keys to adjust the volume and to position the Seek slider.
Enter	Play an item, or select a command or button.
Space	Select or clear a check box.
	To select or clear contiguous check boxes, press and hold **Shift**, use the arrow keys to highlight the appropriate check boxes, and then press **Space**.
	To select or clear check boxes for multiple items that are not contiguous, press and hold **Ctrl**, use the arrow keys to highlight the check boxes, and then press **Space**.
Tab	Move the pointer to a different area.
Shift+Tab	Move the pointer in the opposite direction.
Ctrl+Tab	Move the focus between the inner and outer areas of the Player.
Shift+F10	Display a shortcut menu for the selected item.
Esc	Close any menu.
Alt+Shift+P	Restore from mini Player mode.

Anchor Window Menu

Alt+F6	Move focus onto anchor, press **Alt** key again to display the anchor window menu.
Ctrl+1	Switch to full mode.
Ctrl+O	Open or play a file.
Ctrl+U	Specify the URL or path to a file.

Copying from a CD

Alt+C	Copy tracks to the hard disc.
Alt+S	Stop copying.
Alt+A	Show names of album tracks to find or update information on the Web. Hide album information.
Alt+I	Display/Hide album information.

Copying to a CD or Other Device

Alt+C	Copy files to CD.
Alt+L	Cancel copying operation.
Del	Delete a selected item.
⇧	Move to the previous item in the list.
⇩	Move to the next item in the list.
F5	Refresh the information in the panes.

File Menu Shortcuts

Alt+F	Display the File menu.
Ctrl+O	Open a file.
Ctrl+U	Specify a URL or path to a file.
Ctrl+W	Close or stop playing a file.
Ctrl+N	Create a new playlist.
Ctrl+D	Edit the current playlist.

| F3 | Search specified locations for digital media files. |
| Alt+F4 | Exit or close the Media Player. |

View Menu Shortcuts

Alt+V	Display the View menu.
Ctrl+1	Switch to full mode.
Ctrl+2	Switch to skin mode.
Ctrl+M	Display menu bar in full mode.
Ctrl+Shift+M	Autohide menu bar in full mode.
Ctrl + I	Capture a DVD image.
Alt+Enter	Display video in full screen.
Alt+1	Zoom at 50%.
Alt+2	Zoom at 100%.
Alt+3	Zoom at 200%.

Using the Help Window

You can use the following keyboard shortcuts in the Media Player Help system, to carry out many common tasks.

F1	Display the Help window.
F6	Switch the cursor between the Help topic pane and the navigation pane (Contents, Search, and Index tabs).
Tab	Select the next hidden text or hyperlink.
Shift+Tab	Select the previous hidden text or hyper-link.
Enter	Perform the action for the selected Show All, Hide All, hidden text, or hyperlink.
Alt+O	Display the Options menu to access any Help toolbar command.
Alt+O then T	Hide or show the pane containing the Contents, Search, and Index tabs.
Alt+O then B	Display the previously viewed topic.

Alt+O then F	Display the next topic in a previously displayed sequence of topics.
Alt+O then H	Return to the specified home page.
Alt+O then S	Stop the Help window from opening a Help topic, such as a Web page.
Alt+O then I	Open the Internet Options dialogue box for Internet Explorer to change accessibility settings.
Alt+O then R	Refresh the topic, such as a Web page.
Alt+O then P	Print all topics in a book or a selected topic only.
Alt+F4	Close the Help window .

Using the Media Library

Alt+I	Display/Hide album information.
Alt+A	Display the Playlists button menu.
Alt+S	Show/hide the Search text box.
Alt+N	Search the Media Library.
Alt+D	Display the Add button menu.
Ctrl+N	Create a new playlist.

Play Menu Shortcuts

Alt+P	Display the Play menu.
Ctrl+P	Play or pause playback.
Ctrl+S	Stop playback.
Ctrl+Shift+G	Use a fast play speed.
Ctrl+Shift+N	Use a normal play speed.
Ctrl+Shift+S	Use a slow play speed.
Ctrl+B	Play the previous item.
Ctrl+F	Play the next item.
Ctrl+Shift+B	Rewind a file.
Ctrl+Shift+F	Fast-forward a file.
Ctrl+H	Shuffle the playlist.

Ctrl+T	Repeat the playlist.
Ctrl+Shift+C	Turn captions and subtitles on or off.
F10	Increase the volume.
F9	Decrease the volume.
F8	Mute volume.
Ctrl+E	Eject CD or DVD.

Player Controls Shortcuts

These shortcuts are for the buttons that are available in the Playback Controls area. They are also available when the Player is in skin mode, depending on the skin.

Ctrl+P	Play or pause a file.
Ctrl+S	Stop playback.
F8	Mute volume.
F9	Decrease the volume.
F10	Increase the volume.
Ctrl+B	Play previous item.
Ctrl+F	Play next item.
Ctrl+Shift+B	Rewind.
Ctrl+Shift+F	Fast-forward.
Ctrl+Shift+G	Play faster than normal speed.
Ctrl+Shift+N	Play at normal speed.
Ctrl+Shift+S	Play slower than normal speed.

Skin Chooser Shortcuts

Alt+A	Apply a skin.
Alt+S	Access and download more skins.
Del	Delete a selected item.

4

Internet Explorer 6

Version: 6.0.2800.1106.xpsp2.030422-1633
Cipher Strength: 128-bit
Product ID:55277-OEM-0013863-69183
Update Versions:; SP1; Q330994; Q824145; Q832894;
Q837009; Q831167;

Internet Explorer 6 is Microsoft's current Web browser, which you can use to carry out most of your Internet activities, especially browsing the World Wide Web. It comes with Microsoft Windows XP as standard, but you can also use it with the following earlier versions of Windows: Windows 98, Windows NT 4.0 with Service Pack SP6a and higher, Windows 2000 and Windows Me.

About Internet Explorer 6

With features such as Auto Image Resizing, Image Toolbar, Media Bar, and Print Preview, Explorer 6 makes it easy to manage, save, and print pictures and other media from Web pages. Features such as Favorites, Auto Complete, History, and a Search Companion help you quickly find what you need online.

Explorer 6 has tools to give you security and privacy preferences while on the Internet. You can manage 'cookies' to help control the personal information that Web sites collect about you, use Security Zones to set different levels of security for different sites on the Web, and use Content Advisor to help block access to objectionable content.

Keyboard Shortcuts

The following keyboard actions are the standard shortcuts for working with Internet Explorer 6.

Viewing Web Pages

F1	Open Explorer Help.
F11	Toggle full-screen view.
Tab	Move forward through object items.
Sh+Tab	Move backward through object items.
Alt+Home	Go to Home page.
Alt+⇨	Go to the next page.
Alt+⇦	Go to the previous page.
Sh+F10	Display shortcut menu for link.
F6	Move forward between frames.
Sh+Ctrl+Tab	Move back between frames.
⇧	Scroll up a document.
⇩	Scroll down a document.
PgUp	Large scroll up a document.
PgDn	Large scroll down a document.
Home	Move to the beginning of a document.
End	Move to the end of a document.
Ctrl+F	Find on this page.
F5	Refresh Web page if necessary.
Ctrl+F5	Refresh Web page if necessary or not.
Esc	Stop downloading a page.
Ctrl+O	Go to a new location.
Ctrl+N	Open a new window.
Ctrl+W	Close the current window.
Ctrl+S	Save the current page.
Ctrl+P	Print the current page or active frame.
Enter	Activate a selected link.
Ctrl+E	Open Search in Explorer bar.

Ctrl+I	Open Favorites in Explorer bar.
Ctrl+H	Open History in Explorer bar.
Ctrl+click	Open multiple folders (History/Favorites).

Using the Address bar

Alt+D	Select text in the Address bar.
F4	Display Address bar history.
Ctrl+ ⇐	Move cursor left to next '.' or '/'.
Ctrl+ ⇒	Move cursor right to next '.' or '/'.
Ctrl+Enter	Add 'www.' and '.com' to typed text.
⇑	Move up AutoComplete list.
⇓	Move down AutoComplete list.

Working with Favorites

Ctrl+D	Add page to Favorites.
Ctrl+B	Open Organize Favorites box.
Alt+ ⇑	Move item up Favorites list.
Alt+ ⇓	Move item down Favorites list.

Editing

Ctrl+X	Cut to the Clipboard.
Ctrl+C	Copy to the Clipboard.
Ctrl+V	Insert Clipboard contents.
Ctrl+A	Select all items on Web page.

Using Print Preview

Alt+P	Set printing options and print the page.
Alt+U	Change page settings.
Alt+Home	Display first page to be printed.

Alt+ ⇐	Display previous page to be printed.
Alt+A	Type number of page to be displayed.
Alt+ ⇒	Display the next page to be printed.
Alt+End	Display the last page to be printed.
Alt+Minus (-)	Zoom out.
Alt+Plus (+)	Zoom in.
Alt+Z	Display a list of zoom percentages.
Alt+F	Specify how to print frames.
Alt+C	Close Print Preview.

If you would like more detail on actually using Internet Explorer 6, then may we suggest you keep a lookout for our book BP513, *Internet Explorer 6 and Outlook Express 6 explained*, also published by BERNARD BABANI (publishing) Ltd.

5

Outlook Express 6

Internet Explorer 6 comes with the very powerful e-mail and news facility, Outlook Express 6, built into it, which makes it very easy for you to send and receive e-mail messages. We are impressed with Outlook Express and have used it for our e-mail correspondence.

Uses of Outlook Express

As well as sending and receiving e-mails, you can use Outlook Express for accessing Newsgroups. These are often known as Usenet groups and consist of many thousands of separate news groups which let you actively take part in discussion on a vast number of topics. In fact almost any subject you could think of is covered, and the number of groups is growing larger all the time.

Outlook Express is a program you can use for viewing, and posting (or mailing), messages to these Newsgroups. Unlike e-mail, which is usually 'one-to-one', newsgroups could be said to be 'one-to-many'.

Keyboard Shortcuts

The following keyboard actions are the standard shortcuts for working with Outlook Express 6.

General

F1	Open Help topics.
Ctrl+A	Select all messages.

Main Mail Window

Ctrl+O	Open the selected message.
Ctrl+Q	Mark a message as read.
Tab	Move between window panes.

Main and Read Message Windows

Ctrl+D	Delete a message.
Ctrl+F	Forward a message.
Ctrl+I	Go to your Inbox.
Ctrl+M	Send and receive mail.
Ctrl+N	Open a new message.
Ctrl+P	Print the selected message.
Ctrl+R	Reply to the message author.
Sh+Ctrl+R	Reply to all.
Ctrl+U	Go to next unread message.
Ctrl+ ⇒	Go to next message in the list.
Ctrl+ ⇐	Go to previous message in the list.
Alt+Enter	View properties of selected message.
Sht+Ctrl+B	Open Address Book.
Ctrl+Y	Go to folder.

New Message Window

F3	Find text.
F7	Check spelling.
Esc	Close a message.
Ctrl+K	Check names.
Ctrl+Enter	Send a message.
Sh+Ctrl+S	Add a signature.
Alt+S	Send a message.

Main News Window

Sh+Ctrl+A	Mark all news messages as read.
Ctrl+J	Go to next unread newsgroup.
Sh+Ctrl+M	Download news for offline reading.
Ctrl+O	Open the selected message.
Ctrl+Q	Mark a message as read.
Ctrl+W	Go to a newsgroup.
Ctrl+Y	Go to a folder.
Tab	Move between window panes.
⇐ or +	Expand a news thread.
⇒ or -	Collapse a news thread.

Main and Read Message News Windows

F5	Refresh headers and articles.
Ctrl+F	Forward a message.
Ctrl+G	Reply to all.
Ctrl+N	Post new message to the newsgroup.
Ctrl+P	Print the selected message.
Ctrl+R	Reply to the author.
Ctrl+⇒	Go to the next message in the list.
Ctrl+⇐	Go to previous message in the list.
Alt+Enter	View properties of selected message.
Sh+Ctrl+U	Go to next unread conversation.

New Message Window

Sh+Ctrl+F	Find text.
Esc	Close a message.
Ctrl+K	Check names.
Alt+S	Send a message.
F7	Check spelling.

If you would like more detail on actually using Outlook Express 6, then may we suggest you keep a lookout for our book BP513, *Internet Explorer 6 and Outlook Express 6 explained*, also published by BERNARD BABANI (publishing) Ltd.

6

Microsoft Office 2003

Microsoft Office 2003 is an integrated collection of powerful, full-featured, programs (or applications) with the same look and feel that work together as if they were a single program.

The individual applications which make up *Office 2003* are designed to have the same look and feel, which makes them easy to learn. For example, the majority of menus, toolbar buttons, and dialogue boxes are the same in each application, which gives them a consistent user interface. The Office suite was specifically designed to allow you to quickly and efficiently work with your information data, either on your own or sharing it with others.

The keyboard shortcuts however are not the same throughout the range of Office applications, due to their differing program functions. In this chapter we list the shortcuts that apply to the whole of Office 2003.

Later chapters cover shortcuts specific to the following Office application programs. Please note that not all of these are included in every version of Office 2003!

Outlook 2003 - e-mail and personal information program.
Word 2003 - the 'ultimate' word processor.
Excel 2003 - spreadsheet and graphing application.
Access 2003 - powerful relational database.
Publisher 2003 - a desktop publishing program.
Powerpoint 2003 - a graphics presentation package.
Frontpage 2003 - Web page creation software.

The Help System

The Office 2003 Help System consists of two parts:

- The Help task pane appears as part of the Office application but provides access to all Office Help content.

- The Help window displays topics and other Help content and appears as a window separate from the application.

Help Task Pane

F1	Display the Help task pane.
F6	Switch between the Help task pane and the Office application.
Tab	Select the next item in the Help task pane.
Shift+Tab	Select the previous item in the Help task pane.
Enter	Perform the action for the selected item.
⇓	Select the next item in a table of contents
⇑	Select the previous item in a table of contents.
⇒	Expand the selected item in a table of contents.
⇐	Collapse the selected item in a table of contents.
Alt+⇐	Move back to the previous task pane.
Alt+⇒	Move forward to the next task pane.
Ctrl+Space	Open the menu of task panes.
Ctrl+F1	Close and reopen the current task pane.
⇒	Expand a +/- list.
⇐	Collapse a +/- list.

Help Window

Tab	Select the next hidden text or hyperlink, or Show All or Hide All when used at the top of a topic.
Shift+Tab	Select the previous hidden text or hyper-link, or the **Browser View** button at the top of a Microsoft Office Web site article.
Enter	Perform the action for the selected Show All, Hide All, hidden text, or hyperlink.
Alt+⇐	Move back to the previous Help topic.
Alt+⇒	Move forward to the next Help topic.
Ctrl+P	Print the current Help topic.
⇧ or ⇩	Scroll small amounts up or down within the currently displayed Help topic.
Page Up	Scroll larger amounts up within the currently displayed Help topic.
Page Down	Scroll larger amounts down within the currently displayed Help topic.
Alt+U	Separate the Help window from, or connect it to Word.
Shift+F10	Display a menu for the Help window when the focus is in the Help window.

Menus and Toolbars

You can use the keyboard to select any menu command on an application menu bar. Press **Alt** to select the menu bar, then press the letter that is underlined in the menu name that contains the command you want. In the sub-menu that appears, press the letter underlined in the command name that you want. The following shortcuts are also available:

F10 or Alt	Select the menu bar, or close an open menu and sub-menu at the same time.
Tab	Select the next button or menu, when a toolbar or menu bar is selected.

Shift+Tab	Select the previous button or menu, when a toolbar or menu bar is selected.
Enter	Open the selected menu, or action the selected button or command.
Shift+F10	Display the shortcut, or right-click menu for the selected item.
Alt+Space	Display the title bar shortcut menu.
⇓ or ⇑	Select the next or previous command in an open menu.
⇐ or ⇒	Select the menu to the left or right in the menu bar. When a sub-menu is open, switch between the main menu and the sub-menu.
Home	Select the first command on the menu or sub-menu.
End	Select the last command on the menu or sub-menu.
Esc	Close an open menu or sub-menu.
Shift+⇓	Open the selected menu.
Ctrl+⇓	Expand a shortened menu to display the full set of commands.

Accessing and Using Task Panes

Task panes were introduced in the previous Office XP. They are window panes usually located on the right side of the Office application window, that provide relevant groups of commonly used commands. As long as your screen is large enough, you can use these commands while still working on your documents.

Ctrl+F1	Open the task pane or hide the current task pane.
F6	Move to a task pane from another pane in the program window. (This may need several tries.)

Ctrl+Tab	When a menu or toolbar is active, move to a task pane. (You may need to press **Ctrl+Tab** more than once.)
Ctrl+Space	Open a menu of task panes.
Alt+Home	Go to the Getting Started task pane.
Alt+⇐	Reverse the sequence of task panes you opened.
Alt+⇒	Repeat the sequence of task panes you opened.
Esc	Close a menu if one is currently open, or go back to the document.
Tab	Select the next option in the active task pane.
Shift+Tab	Select the previous option in the active task pane.
⇓ or ⇑	Move among choices in a selected sub-menu; move among certain options in a group of options.
Space or Enter	Open the selected menu, or perform the action assigned to the selected button.
Shift+F10	Open a shortcut menu in a document.
Home or End	Select the first or last command on the menu or sub-menu.
Page Up	Scroll up in the selected gallery list.
Page Down	Scroll down in the selected gallery list.
Ctrl+⇒	Expand an item in the gallery list.
Ctrl+⇐	Collapse an item in the gallery list.
Ctrl+Home	Move to the top of the selected gallery list.
Ctrl+End	Move to the bottom of the selected gallery list.

Selecting Menus, Toolbars and Task Panes

Alt   Select the menu bar.

Ctrl+Tab   (Repeatedly) - Select a toolbar or the task pane.

Re-sizing and Moving Toolbars

Ctrl+ Space   Displays the Toolbar Options menu when the Toolbar is selected.

To re-size the toolbar select the **Size** command, press **Enter** and use the arrow keys. Press **Ctrl+arrow** to resize one pixel at a time.

To move the toolbar select the **Move** command, press **Enter** and use the arrow keys to position the toolbar. Press **Ctrl+arrow** to move one pixel at a time.

Re-sizing and Moving Task Panes

Ctrl+ Space   Displays a menu of additional commands when the task pane is selected.

To re-size the task pane use the ⇩ key to select the **Size** command, press **Enter** and use the arrow keys to re-size the task pane. Use **Ctrl+arrow** keys to re-size by one pixel at a time.

To move the task pane use the ⇩ key to select the **Move** command, press **Enter** and use the arrow keys to position the task pane. Use **Ctrl+arrow** keys to move by one pixel at a time.

When you are finished moving or re-sizing, press **Esc** or **Enter**.

Using Dialogue Boxes

Alt+F6	Move from an open dialogue box back to the document. Used for dialogue boxes such as Find and Replace.
Tab	Move to the next option or option group.
Shift+Tab	Move to the previous option or option group.
Ctrl+Tab	Switch to the next tab in a dialogue box.
Ctrl+Shift+Tab	Switch to the previous tab in a dialogue box.
Arrow keys	Move between dialogue box options.
Space	Perform the action assigned to the selected button; check or clear the selected check box.
Alt+⇓	Open a selected drop-down list.
Esc	Close a selected drop-down list; cancel a command and close a dialogue box.
Enter	Run the selected command.

Edit Boxes in Dialogue Boxes

An edit box is a blank in which you type or paste an entry, such as an instruction, filename or path.

Home	Move to the beginning of the entry.
End	Move to the end of the entry.
⇐ or ⇒	Move one character to the left or right.
Ctrl+⇐	Move one word to the left.
Ctrl+⇒	Move one word to the right.
Shift+⇐	Select/unselect one character to the left.
Shift+⇒	Select/unselect one character to the right.
Ctrl+Shift+⇐	Select/unselect one word to the left.
Ctrl+Shift+⇒	Select/unselect one word to the right.
Shift+Home	Select from the insertion point to the beginning of the entry.
Shift+End	Select from the insertion point to the end of the entry.

Open, Save As and Insert Picture Boxes

Ctrl+F12	Display the Open dialogue box.
F12	Display the Save As dialogue box.
Alt+1	Go to the previous folder (⚫ button).
Alt+2	Open the folder up one level from the open folder (🗂 button).
Alt+3	Close the dialogue box and open Web search page (🔎 button).
Alt+4	Delete the selected folder or file (✕ button).
Alt+5	Create a new sub-folder in the open folder (📁 button).
Alt+6	Switch between List, Details, Properties, Preview Thumbnails, Tiles, and Icons views (▦ button).
Alt+7 or Alt+L	Show the Tools menu.
Shift+F10	Display a shortcut menu for a selected item such as a folder or file.
Tab	Move between options or areas in the dialogue box.
F4 or Alt+I	Open the Look in or Save in list.
F5	Update the files visible in the Open or Save As dialogue box.

If you would like more detail on actually using Office 2003, then may we suggest you keep a lookout for our book BP544, *Microsoft Office 2003 explained*, also published by BERNARD BABANI (publishing) Ltd.

7

Microsoft Outlook 2003

Outlook 2003 is both a powerful e-mail program and a personal information manager (PIM) - like an electronic Filofax - that supports a full set of multi-user, group scheduling functions. Outlook can be made the centre of activity for all the other Office 2003 applications, and it can be used *online* or *off-line*.

Overview

Outlook provides an integrated solution for managing and organising e-mail and Newsgroup messages, schedules, tasks, notes, contacts, and other information. It provides easy access to your Contacts, Calendar, Tasks, Folders, Shortcuts, and Journal so you can find the information you need to answer e-mail messages, schedule appointments, and finish projects. All in all a very useful program, which we now both use.

Like the other applications in Office 2003, Outlook has an incredible number of keyboard shortcuts. We have tried to rationalise these here.

Note: When a key from the numeric keypad (on the right of a standard keyboard) is needed we precede it with **Num**.

Keyboard Shortcuts

The following keyboard actions are the standard shortcuts for working with Outlook 2003. Most of the shortcuts for Office 2003, listed in Chapter 6, are available as well.

Basic Navigation

Ctrl+1	Switch to Mail.
Ctrl+2	Switch to Calendar.
Ctrl+3	Switch to Contacts.
Ctrl+4	Switch to Tasks.
Ctrl+5	Switch to Notes.
Ctrl+6	Switch to Folder List in Navigation Pane.
Ctrl+7	Switch to Shortcuts.
Ctrl+,	Next open item.
Ctrl+.	Previous open item.
F6	Switch between the Folder List and the main Outlook window.
Tab	Move among the Outlook window, the Navigation Pane, and the Reading Pane.
⇐, ⇒, ⇑ or ⇓	Move around within the Navigation Pane.
Ctrl+Y	Go to a different folder.
Plus or Minus	(On the numeric keypad) - Expand or collapse a selected group in the Navigation Pane.
⇐, ⇒	Collapse/expand a group in the e-mail message list.

Creating Items or Files

Ctrl+Shift+A	Create an Appointment.
Ctrl+Shift+C	Create a Contact.
Ctrl+Shift+L	Create a Distribution list.
Ctrl+Shift+X	Create a Fax.
Ctrl+Shift+E	Create a Folder.

Ctrl+Shift+J	Create a Journal entry.
Ctrl+Shift+Q	Create a Meeting request.
Ctrl+Shift+M	Create a Message.
Ctrl+Shift+N	Create a Note.
Ctrl+Shift+H	Create a new Office document.
Ctrl+Shift+S	Post in this folder.
Ctrl+Shift+P	Search Folder.
Ctrl+Shift+K	Create a Task.
Ctrl+Shift+U	Create a Task request.

General to all Tools

Shift+F1	Display ScreenTip for the active element.
Ctrl+S	Save.
Alt+S	Save and Close, Send message.
F12	Save As.
Ctrl+Z	Undo.
Ctrl+D	Delete.
Ctrl+P	Print.
Ctrl+Shift+Y	Copy item.
Ctrl+Shift+V	Move item.
Ctrl+K	Check names in Address Book.
F7	Check spelling.
Ctrl+Shift+G	Flag message for follow-up.
Ctrl+F	Forward.
Ctrl+Enter	Send/post/invite all.
F3 or Ctrl+E	Find items.
F4	Search for text in items.
Shift+F4	Find next during text search.
Ctrl+Shift+F	Use Advanced Find.
Ctrl+Shift+P	Create a new Search Folder.
F2	Turn on editing in a field. (This does not work in icon view).

E-mail Shortcuts

Ctrl+Shift+I	Switch to Inbox.
Ctrl+Shift+O	Switch to Outbox.
Ctrl+Enter	Send.
Ctrl+R	Reply to a message.
Ctrl+ Alt+J	Mark a message as not junk.
Ctrl+Shift+I	Display blocked external content in a message.
Ctrl+ Shift+S	Post to a folder.
Ctrl+M or F9	Check for new mail.
⇧	Go to the next message.
⇩	Go to the previous message.
Alt+ ⇧	Go to the row above (message or group heading).
Alt+ ⇩	Go to the row below (message or group heading).
Ctrl+N	Compose a new message.
Ctrl+O	Open a received message.
Ctrl+Shift+B	Display the Address Book.
Ctrl+Shift+O	Convert an HTML or RTF message to plain text.
Insert	Add a Quick Flag to a message.
Ctrl+Shift+G	Display the Flag for Follow Up dialogue box.
Ctrl+Q	Mark as read.

Calendar Shortcuts

Alt+C	Accept.
Alt+D	Decline.

Contacts Shortcuts

Ctrl+Shift+D	Dial.
F11	Enter a name in the Find a Contact box.

Shortcuts for Tasks

Alt+C	Accept.
Alt+D	Decline.

Print Preview

Ctrl+F2	Open print preview.
Alt+P	Print a print preview.
Alt+S or Alt+U	Print preview page setup.
Alt+Z	Zoom.
Alt+C	Close print preview.

Send/Receive

F9	Starts a send/receive for all defined Send/Receive groups. This can include headers, full items, specified folders, items less than a specific size, or any combination that you have defined.
Shift+F9	Starts a send/receive for the current folder, retrieving full items (header, item, and any attachments).

Formatting Text

Alt+O	Display the Format menu.
Shift+F3	Switch case of selected text.
Ctrl+B	Make text bold.
Ctrl+Shift+L	Add bullets.
Ctrl+I	Add italics.
Ctrl+T	Increase indent.
Ctrl+Shift+T	Decrease indent.
Ctrl+L	Left align text.
Ctrl+E	Centre align text.
CRTL+U	Underline.
Ctrl+]	Increase font size.
Ctrl+[	Decrease font size.
Ctrl+X	Cut selection to clipboard.
Ctrl+C	Copy selection to clipboard.
Ctrl+V	Paste current clipboard contents.
Ctrl+Shift+Z	Clear formatting.

Different Outlook Views

Table View

For general use

Enter	Open an item.
Ctrl+A	Select all items.
Page Down	Go to the item at the bottom of the screen.
Page Up	Go to the item at the top of the screen.

Shift+⇑ or Shift+⇓	Extend or reduce the selected items by one item.
Ctrl+⇑ or Ctrl+⇓	Go to the next or previous item without extending the selection.
Ctrl+Space	Select or unselect the active item.
Ctrl+Home	Move every item in the selection to the top of the list order.
Ctrl+End	Move every item in the selection to the bottom of the list order.

When a group is selected

Enter or ⇒	Expand the group.
Enter or ⇐	Collapse the group.
⇑	Select the previous group.
⇓	Select the next group.
Home	Select the first group.
End	Select the last group.
Num-	Collapses the group.
Num+	Expands the group.
⇒	Select the first item on screen in an expanded group or the first item off screen to the right.

For all groups

Ctrl+Num-	Collapses all groups.
Ctrl+Num+	Expands all groups.

Day/Week/Month View

Working in all three views

Alt+1 to 9	View from 1 through 9 days.
Alt+0	View 10 days.
Alt+hyphen	Switch to weeks view.

Alt+=	Switch to months view.
Ctrl+Tab or F6	Move between Calendar, TaskPad, and the Folder List.
Shift+Tab	Select the previous appointment.
⇐	Go to the previous day.
⇒	Go to the next day.
Alt+ ⇐	Move selected item to the previous day when multiple days appear.
Alt+ ⇒	Move selected item to the next day when multiple days appear.
Alt+ ⇓	Go to the same day in the next week .
Alt+ ⇑	Go to the same day in the previous week.

Working in Day View

Home	Select the time that begins your work day.
End	Select the time that ends your work day.
⇑	Select the previous block of time.
⇓	Select the next block of time.
Page Up	Select the block of time at the top of the screen.
Page Down	Select the block of time at the bottom of the screen.
Shift+ ⇑ or ⇓	Extend or reduce the selected time
Alt+ ⇑ or ⇓	Move an appointment when the cursor is in the appointment.
Alt+Shift+ ⇑ or ⇓	Change an appointment start or end time when the cursor is in the appointment.
Alt+ ⇓	Move selected item to the same day in the next week.
Alt+ ⇑	Move selected item to the same day in the previous week.

Working in Week or Month Views

Home	Go to the first day of the week.
End	Go to the last day of the week.
Page Up	Go to the same day of the week in the previous week (or 5 weeks previous if viewing by month).
Page Down	Go to the same day of the week in the next week (or 5 weeks ahead if viewing by month).
Alt+Arrow	Move the appointment up, down, left, or right.
Shift+Arrow	Change the duration of the selected block of time.

Date Navigator

Alt+Home	Go to the first day of the current week.
Alt+End	Go to the last day of the current week.
Alt+⇧	Go to the same day in the previous week.
Alt+⇩	Go to the same day in the next week.
Alt+Page Up	Go to the first day of the month.
Alt+Page Down	Go to the last day of the month.

Address Card View

For general use

xx	Select a specific card in the list.
⇧	Select the previous card.
⇩	Select the next card.
Home	Select the first card in the list.
End	Select the last card in the list.
Page Up	Select the first card on the current page.
Page Down	Select the first card on the next page.

⇨	Select the closest card in the next column.
⇦	Select the closest card in the previous column
Ctrl+Space	Select or unselect the active card.
Shift+ ⇧	Extend the selection to the previous card and unselect cards after the starting point.
Shift+ ⇩	Extend the selection to the next card and unselect cards before the starting point .
Ctrl+Shift+ ⇧	Extend the selection to the previous card, regardless of the starting point.
Ctrl+Shift+ ⇩	Extend the selection to the next card, regardless of the starting point.
Shift+Home	Extend the selection to the first card in the list.
Shift+End	Extend the selection to the last card in the list.
Shift+Page Up	Extend the selection to the first card on the previous page.
Shift+Page Down	Extend the selection to the last card on the last page.

As long as a card is selected by clicking its heading, you can use the following shortcuts to move between cards without changing the selection.

Ctrl+ ⇩	Move to the next card.
Ctrl+ ⇧	Move to the previous card.
Ctrl+Home	Move to the first card in the list.
Ctrl+End	Move to the last card in the list.
Ctrl+Page Up	Move to the first card on the previous page.
Ctrl+Page Down	Move to the first card on the next page.
Ctrl+ ⇦	Move to the closest card in the previous column.

Ctrl+⇨	Move to the closest card in the next column.
F2	Move to a field in the active card.

You can use the following shortcuts to move between fields in a card. A field in a card must be selected by clicking it or by pressing the F2 key.

Tab	Move to the next field, or to the first field in the next card.
Shift+Tab	Move to the previous field, or to the last field in the previous card.
Enter	Move to the next field, or add a line to a multi-line field.
Shift+Enter	Move to the previous field without leaving the active card.
F2	Display the insertion point in the active field to edit text.

You can use the following shortcuts to move between characters in a field. Again a field in a card must be selected by clicking it or by pressing the F2 key.

Enter	Add a line in a multi-line field.
Home	Move to the beginning of a line.
End	Move to the end of a line.
Page Up	Move to the beginning of a multi-line field.
Page Down	Move to the end of a multi-line field.
⇧	Move to the previous line in a multi-line field.
⇩	Move to the next line in a multi-line field.
⇦	Move to the previous character in a field.
⇨	Move to the next character in a field.

Timeline View

When an item is selected

⇐	Select the previous item.
⇒	Select the next item.
Shift+⇐ or Shift+⇒	Select several adjacent items.
Ctrl+⇐+Space	Select several non-adjacent items.
Ctrl+⇒+Space	Select several non-adjacent items.
Enter	Open the selected items.
Page Up	Display the items one screen above the items on screen.
Page Down	Display the items one screen below the items on screen.
Home	Select the first item on the timeline, or the first item in a group.
End	Select the last item on the timeline, or the last item in a group.
Ctrl+Home	Display (without selecting) the first item on the timeline, or the first item in a group.
Ctrl+End	Display (without selecting) the last item on the timeline, or the last item in a group.

When a group is selected

Enter or ⇒	Expand the group.
Enter or ⇐	Collapse the group.
⇑	Select the previous group.
⇓	Select the next group.
Home	Select the first group on the timeline.
End	Select the last group on the timeline.
⇒	Select the first item on screen in an expanded group or the first item off screen to the right.

When a unit of time is selected

⇐	Move back in increments of time that are the same as those shown on the time scale.
⇒	Move forward in increments of time that are the same as those shown on the time scale.
Shift+Tab	When the lower time scale is selected, select the upper time scale.
Tab	When the upper time scale is selected, select the lower time scale.
Tab	When the lower time scale is selected, select the first item on screen or the first group on screen if items are grouped.

If you would like more detail on actually using Outlook 2003, then may we suggest you keep a lookout for our book BP544, *Microsoft Office 2003 explained*, also published by BERNARD BABANI (publishing) Ltd.

8

Microsoft Word 2003

Microsoft's Word 2003 is part of the Office 2003 package and is without doubt the most powerful Windows word processor so far. As you would expect, it is fully integrated with all the other Office 2003 applications.

This version of Word, like its predecessors, has particularly strong leanings towards desk top publishing which offers fully editable WYSIWYG (**w**hat **y**ou **s**ee **i**s **w**hat **y**ou **g**et) modes that can be viewed in various zoom levels. Couple this with the ability to include and manipulate full colour graphics and to easily create Web pages and you can see the enormous power of the program.

In short this is a word processor that offers almost every imaginable feature, including background spelling and grammar checking, integrated drawing tools, Smart Tags and Task Panes. The new version also includes enhanced merge and markup capabilities.

The package has an incredible number of keyboard shortcuts. In the following pages we first list what we think are the most useful to remember, and then follow with the rest, divided into the different aspects of Word. The function key combinations are then listed together. We suggest you browse the listings and only attempt to memorise the shortcuts that are most useful to you.

Quick Reference

Shortcuts for some of the more common tasks done in a Microsoft Word document.

Ctrl+Shift+Space	Create a non-breaking space.
Ctrl+Hyphen	Create a non-breaking hyphen.
Ctrl+B	Make selected text bold.
Ctrl+I	Make selected text italic.
Ctrl+U	Underline selected text.
Ctrl+Shift+<	Decrease font size.
Ctrl+Shift+>	Increase font size.
Ctrl+Space	Remove paragraph or character formatting.
Ctrl+C	Copy the selected text or object.
Ctrl+X	Cut the selected text or object.
Ctrl+V	Paste text or an object.
Ctrl+Z	Undo the last action.
Ctrl+Y	Redo the last action.

Working with Documents

Manipulating Files

Ctrl+N	Create a new document of the same type as the current or most recent one.
Ctrl+O	Open an existing document.
Ctrl+W	Close a document.
Alt+Ctrl+S	Split the document window.
Alt+Shift+C	Remove the document window split.
Ctrl+S	Save the current document.

Finding and Replacing Text

Ctrl+F	Find text, formatting, and special items.
Alt+Ctrl+Y	Repeat a find operation, after closing the Find and Replace window.
Ctrl+H	Replace text, specific formatting, and special items.
Ctrl+G	Go to a page, bookmark, footnote, table, comment, graphic, or other location.

Undo and Redo Actions

Esc	Cancel an action.
Ctrl+Z	Undo an action.
Ctrl+Y	Redo or repeat an action.

Switching Views

Alt+Ctrl+P	Switch to Print Layout view (headers, footnotes, columns, and text boxes appear in their actual positions).
Alt+Ctrl+O	Switch to Outline view.

Alt+Ctrl+N	Switch to Normal view (showing text formatting and a simplified page layout).
Alt+R	Switch to Reading view.
Ctrl+\	Expand or collapse sub-documents in a master document.

Using Outline View

When in Outline view the following shortcuts are available.

Alt+Shift+ ⇐	Promote a paragraph.
Alt+Shift+ ⇒	Demote a paragraph.
Ctrl+Shift+N	Demote to body text.
Alt+Shift+ ⇑	Move selected paragraphs up.
Alt+Shift+ ⇓	Move selected paragraphs down.
Alt+Shift+plus (+)	Expand text under a heading.
Alt+Shift+minus (-)	Collapse text under a heading.
Alt+Shift+A	Expand or collapse all text or headings.
/ (numeric keypad)	Hide or display character formatting.
Alt+Shift+L	Show the first line of body text or all of body text.
Alt+Shift+1	Show all headings with the Heading 1 style.
Alt+Shift+n	Show all headings up to Heading n.
Ctrl+Tab	Insert a tab character.

Printing and Previewing Documents

Ctrl+P	Print a document.
Alt+Ctrl+I	Switch print preview on or off.
Arrows	Move around the preview page when zoomed in.
Page Up	Move up one preview page when zoomed out.
Page Down	Move down one preview page when zoomed out.

| Ctrl+Home | Move to the first preview page when zoomed out. |
| Ctrl+End | Move to the last preview page when zoomed out. |

Reviewing Documents

Alt+Ctrl+M	Insert a comment.
Ctrl+Shift+E	Turn track changes on or off. These show where a deletion, insertion, or other editing change has been made.
Alt+Shift+C	Close the Reviewing Pane if it is open.

Reading Layout View

Home	Go to beginning of document.
End	Go to end of document.
Ctrl+]	Increase the size of selected text by one point.
Ctrl+[	Decrease the size of selected text by one point.
Esc	Exit reading layout view.

References, Footnotes, and Endnotes

Alt+Shift+O	Mark a table of contents entry.
Alt+Shift+I	Mark a table of authorities entry.
Alt+Shift+X	Mark an index entry.
Alt+Ctrl+F	Insert a footnote.
Alt+Ctrl+D	Insert an endnote.

Working with Web Pages

Some of these require the Web toolbar to be showing.

Ctrl+K	Insert a hyperlink.
Alt+ ⇐	Go back one page.
Alt+ ⇒	Go forward one page.
F9	Refresh.

Navigating and Editing Text

Moving the Insertion Point

⇐	Move one character to the left.
⇒	Move one character to the right.
Ctrl+ ⇐	Move one word to the left.
Ctrl+ ⇒	Move one word to the right.
Ctrl+ ⇑	Move one paragraph up.
Ctrl+ ⇓	Move one paragraph down.
Shift+Tab	Move one cell to the left in a table.
Tab	Move one cell to the right in a table.
⇑	Move up one line.
⇓	Move down one line.
End	Move to the end of a line.
Home	To the beginning of a line.
Alt+Ctrl+Page Up	To the top of the window.
Alt+Ctrl+Page Dn	To the end of the window.
Page Up	Scroll up one screen.
Page Dn	Scroll down one screen.
Ctrl+Page Dn	Move to the top of the next page.
Ctrl+Page Up	Move to the top of the previous page.
Ctrl+End	Move to the end of a document.
Ctrl+Home	Move to the beginning of a document.
Shift+F5	Move to a previous revision.

Deleting, Copying and Moving

Backspace	Delete one character to the left.
Ctrl+Backspace	Delete one word to the left.
Delete	Delete one character to the right.
Ctrl+Delete	Delete one word to the right.
Ctrl+X	Cut selected text to the clipboard.
Ctrl+Z	Undo the last action.
Ctrl+C	Copy selection to the clipboard.
Ctrl+C, Ctrl+C	Display the Office clipboard.
Ctrl+V	Paste the clipboard contents.
Alt+Shift+R	Copy the header or footer used in the previous section of the document.

Inserting Special Characters

Ctrl+F9	Insert a field.
Shift+Enter	Insert a line break, but stay in the same paragraph.
Ctrl+Enter	Insert a page break.
Ctrl+Shift+Enter	Insert a section break.
Alt+Ctrl+minus	Insert an 'em' dash.
Ctrl+minus	Insert an 'en' dash.
Ctrl+Shift+minus	Insert a nonbreaking hyphen.
Ctrl+Shift+Space	Insert a nonbreaking space.
Alt+Ctrl+C	Insert the copyright symbol.
Alt+Ctrl+R	Insert the registered trademark symbol.
Alt+Ctrl+T	Insert the trademark symbol.
Alt+Ctrl+.	Insert an ellipsis.
Ctrl+,	Insert a single opening quotation mark, when placed in front of a word.
Ctrl+,	Insert a single closing quotation mark, when placed behind a word.
Ctrl+', Shift+'	Insert double opening quotation marks, when placed in front of a word.
Ctrl+', Shift+'	Insert double closing quotation marks, when placed behind a word.

Character and Paragraph Formatting

Ctrl+Shift+C	Copy formatting from text.
Ctrl+Shift+V	Apply the copied formatting to text.
Ctrl+Shift+F	Activates the Font box on the Format toolbar, so you can change the font.
Ctrl+Shift+P	Activates the Font Size box on the Format toolbar, so you can change the font size.
Ctrl+Shift+>	Increase the font size.
Ctrl+Shift+<	Decrease the font size.
Ctrl+]	Increase the font size by 1 point.
Ctrl+[	Decrease the font size by 1 point.
Ctrl+D	Opens the Font dialogue box so you can change the formatting of characters.
Shift+F3	Change the case of letters between upper, lower and title case.
Ctrl+Shift+A	Format letters as all capitals.
Ctrl+B	Apply bold formatting.
Ctrl+U	Underline selected text.
Ctrl+Shift+W	Underline words but not spaces.
Ctrl+Shift+D	Double-underline text.
Ctrl+Shift+H	Apply hidden text formatting.
Ctrl+I	Apply italic formatting.
Ctrl+Shift+K	Format letters as small capitals.
Ctrl+=	Apply subscript formatting.
Ctrl+plus	Apply superscript formatting.
Ctrl+Space	Remove manual character formatting.
Ctrl+Shift+Q	Change the selection to the Symbol font.
Ctrl+Shift+*	Display non-printing characters.
Ctrl+1	Set line spacing to single-space.
Ctrl+2	Set line spacing to double-space.
Ctrl+5	Set line spacing to 1.5 spacing.
Ctrl+0	Add or remove one line space preceding a paragraph.

Ctrl+E	Centre the current paragraph.
Ctrl+J	Justify the current paragraph.
Ctrl+L	Left align the current paragraph.
Ctrl+R	Right align the current paragraph.
Ctrl+M	Left indent a paragraph.
Ctrl+Shift+M	Remove a left paragraph indent.
Ctrl+T	Create a hanging indent.
Ctrl+Shift+T	Reduce a hanging indent.
Ctrl+Q	Remove paragraph formatting.
Ctrl+Shift+S	Activates the Style box on the Format toolbar, so you can apply a style.
Alt+Ctrl+K	Start AutoFormat.
Ctrl+Shift+N	Apply the Normal style.
Alt+Ctrl+1	Apply the Heading 1 style.
Alt+Ctrl+2	Apply the Heading 2 style.
Alt+Ctrl+3	Apply the Heading 3 style.
Ctrl+Shift+L	Apply the List style.

Working in Word Tables

Tab	Move to the next cell in the row and select its contents.
Shift+Tab	Move to the preceding cell in a row and select its contents.
Shift+F8	Remove the selection.
Alt+Home	Move to the first cell in a row.
Alt+End	Move to the last cell in a row.
Alt+Page Up	Move to the first cell in a column.
Alt+Page Down	Move to the last cell in a column.
⇧	Move to the previous row.
⇩	Move to the next row.
Enter	Insert a new paragraph in a cell.
Ctrl+Tab	Insert a tab character in a cell.

Using Mail Merge

Before using these commands you must start the Mail Merge task pane with the **Tools**, **Letters and Mailings**, **Mail Merge** menu command.

Alt+Shift+K	Preview a mail merge.
Alt+Shift+N	Merge a document.
Alt+Shift+M	Print the merged document.
Alt+Shift+E	Edit a mail-merge data document.
Alt+Shift+F	Insert a merge field.
Alt+Shift+D	Insert a DATE field.
Alt+Ctrl+L	Insert a LISTNUM field.
Alt+Shift+P	Insert a PAGE field.
Alt+Shift+T	Insert a TIME field.
Ctrl+F9	Insert an empty field.

Ctrl+Shift+F7	Update linked information in a Word source document.
F9	Update selected fields.
Ctrl+Shift+F9	Unlink a field.
Shift+F9	Switch between a selected field code and its result.
Alt+F9	Switch between all field codes and their results.
Alt+Shift+F9	Run GOTOBUTTON or MACROBUTTON from the field that displays the field results.
F11	Go to the next field.
Shift+F11	Go to the previous field.
Ctrl+F11	Lock a field.
Ctrl+Shift+F11	Unlock a field.

Sending E-mail Messages

When you are using Word to e-mail a document or message you can use the following keys as long as the insertion point is in the e-mail header. If it isn't, use the Shift+Tab shortcut to move it into the header.

Alt+S	Send the active document or message.
Ctrl+Shift+B	Open the Address Book.
Alt+K, Ctrl+K	Check the names on the To, Cc, and Bcc lines against entries in your Address Book.
Alt+.	Open the Address Book in the To field.
Alt+C	Open the Address Book in the Cc field.
Alt+B	If the Bcc field is visible, open the Address Book in the Bcc field. If the Bcc field is not visible, open the Address Book for any field, and type a name in the Bcc box.

Alt+J	Go to the Subject field.
Alt+P	Open the Microsoft Outlook Message Options dialogue box.
Ctrl+Shift+G	Create a message flag.
Tab	Move the insertion point to the next box in the e-mail header. When the last box is active, this moves the insertion point to the body of the document or message.
Shift+Tab	Select the previous field or button in the e-mail header.

Function Key Combinations

The following listings show many of the Word keyboard shortcuts indexed by the use of the function keys.

F1	Get Help or visit Microsoft Office Online.
F2	Move text or graphics.
F3	Insert an AutoText entry. In Word you can store standard text or graphics you you frequently use as AutoTexts, and this is a quick way of using them.
F4	Repeat the last action.
F5	Choose the **Go To** command on the **Edit** menu.
F6	Go to the next pane or frame.
F7	Choose the **Spelling** command from the **Tools** menu.
F8	Extend a selection.
F9	Update selected fields.
F10	Activate the menu bar.
F11	Go to the next field.
F12	Choose the **Save As** command from the **File** menu.
Shift+F1	Start context-sensitive Help or reveal formatting.
Shift+F2	Copy text.
Shift+F3	Change the case of letters.
Shift+F4	Repeat a **Find** or **Go To** action.
Shift+F5	Move to the last change.
Shift+F6	Go to the previous pane or frame.
Shift+F7	Open the Thesaurus.
Shift+F8	Shrink a selection.
Shift+F9	Switch between a field code and its result.
Shift+F10	Display a shortcut menu.

Shift+F11	Go to the previous field.
Shift+F12	Choose the **Save** command.
Ctrl+F2	Choose the **Print Preview** command.
Ctrl+F3	Cut to the Spike (A special AutoText entry that stores multiple deletions).
Ctrl+F4	Close the window.
Ctrl+F5	Restore the document window size.
Ctrl+F6	Go to the next window.
Ctrl+F7	Choose the **Move** command from the title bar shortcut menu.
Ctrl+F8	Choose the **Size** command from the title bar shortcut menu.
Ctrl+F9	Insert an empty field.
Ctrl+F10	Maximise the document window.
Ctrl+F11	Lock a field.
Ctrl+F12	Choose the **Open** command from the **File** menu.
Ctrl+Shift+F3	Insert the contents of the Spike (A special AutoText entry that stores multiple deletions).
Ctrl+Shift+F5	Edit a bookmark.
Ctrl+Shift+F6	Go to the previous window.
Ctrl+Shift+F7	Update linked information in a Word source document.
Ctrl+Shift+F8	Then press an arrow key to extend a selection or block.
Ctrl+Shift+F9	Unlink a field.
Ctrl+Shift+F11	Unlock a field.
Ctrl+Shift+F12	Choose the Print command.
Alt+F1	Go to the next field.
Alt+F3	Create an AutoText entry.
Alt+F4	Close down Microsoft Word.
Alt+F5	Restore the program window size.

Alt+F6	Move from an open dialogue box back to the document.
Alt+F7	Find the next misspelling or grammatical error. For this to work, the **Check spelling as you type** check box must be selected in the Spelling & Grammar tab of the **Tools**, **Options** dialogue box.
Alt+F8	Run a macro.
Alt+F9	Switch between all field codes and their results.
Alt+F10	Maximise the program window.
Alt+F11	Display Microsoft Visual Basic code.
Alt+Shift+F1	Go to the previous field.
Alt+Shift+F2	Choose the Save command.
Alt+Shift+F9	Run GOTOBUTTON or MACROBUTTON from the field that displays the field results.
Alt+Shift+F10	Display the menu or message for a smart tag. If more than one smart tag is present, switch to the next smart tag and display its menu or message.
Alt+Shift+F11	Start the Microsoft Script Editor.
Ctrl+Alt+F1	Display Microsoft System Information.
Ctrl+Alt+F2	Action the **File**, **Open** menu command.

If you would like more detail on actually using Word 2003, then may we suggest you keep a lookout for our book BP544, *Microsoft Office 2003 explained*, also published by BERNARD BABANI (publishing) Ltd.

9

Microsoft Excel 2003

Microsoft Excel 2003 is a powerful and versatile spreadsheet package which, over the years in its various versions, has proved its usefulness, not only in the business world, but with scientific and engineering users as well.

A spreadsheet's power lies in its ability to emulate everything that can be done with a pencil, paper and a calculator. Its power is derived from the power of the computer it is running on, and the flexibility and accuracy with which it can deal with the solution of the various applications it is programmed to manage. These can vary from record keeping, budgeting and forecasting to the solution of complex scientific and engineering problems.

Excel's Keyboard Shortcuts

Like the other applications in Office 2003, Excel has an incredible number of keyboard shortcuts. We list in this chapter most of the available shortcuts and their specific uses. The last few pages contain Exel's **Ctrl** and function key shortcuts, and some of the other more common ones.

Worksheet and Workbook Shortcuts

Working with Worksheets

Shift+F11	Insert a new worksheet.
Ctrl+Page Down	Move to the next sheet in the workbook.
Ctrl+Page Up	Move to the previous sheet in the workbook.

Moving and Scrolling in Worksheets

⇑, ⇓, ⇐ or ⇒	Move one cell up, down, left, or right.
Tab	Move one cell to the right.
Shift+Tab	Move one cell to the left.
Ctrl+arrow	Move to the edge of the current data region.
Home	Move to the beginning of the row.
Ctrl+Home	Move to the beginning of the worksheet.
Ctrl+End	Move to the last cell on the worksheet, in the bottom-most used row of the right-most used column.
Page Down	Move down one screen.
Page Up	Move up one screen.
Alt+Page Down	Move one screen to the right.
Alt+Page Up	Move one screen to the left.
F6	Switch to the next pane in a worksheet that has been split.
Shift+F6	Switch to the previous pane in a worksheet that has been split.
Ctrl+Backspace	Scroll to display the active cell.
F5	Display the Go To dialogue box.
Shift+F5	Display the Find dialogue box.
Shift+F4	Repeat the last Find action.
Tab	Move between unlocked cells on a protected worksheet.

Moving in a Selected Range

Enter	Move from top to bottom within the selected range.
Shift+Enter	Move from bottom to top within the selected range.
Tab	Move from left to right within the selected range. If cells in a single column are selected, move down.
Shift+Tab	Move from right to left within the selected range. If cells in a single column are selected, move up.
Ctrl+.	Move clockwise to the next corner of the selected range.
Ctrl+Alt+⇒	In non-adjacent selections, switch to the next selection to the right.
Ctrl+Alt+⇐	Switch to the next non-adjacent selection to the left.

Moving and Scrolling in End Mode

'End' appears in the status bar when End mode is selected, as below.

End	Turn End mode on or off.
End+arrow	Move by one block of data within a row or column.
End+Home	Move to the last cell on the worksheet, in the bottom-most used row of the right-most used column.
End+Enter	Move to the rightmost non-blank cell in the current row.

When Scroll Lock is On

Scroll Lock	Turn Scroll Lock off or back on.

Home	Move to the cell in the upper-left corner of the window.
End	Move to the cell in the lower-right corner of the window.
⇧ or ⇩	Scroll one row up or down.
⇦ or ⇨	Scroll one column left or right.

Selecting Data and Cells

Cells, Rows, Columns, and Objects

Ctrl+Space	Select the entire column.
Shift+Space	Select the entire row.
Ctrl+A	Select the entire worksheet.
Shift+Backspace	With multiple cells selected, select only the active cell.
Ctrl+Shift+Space	With an object selected, select all objects on a sheet.
Ctrl+6	Alternate between hiding objects, displaying objects, and displaying placeholders for objects.

Cells with Specific Characteristics

Ctrl+Shift+*	Select the current region around the active cell (the data area enclosed by blank rows and blank columns).
Ctrl+/	Select the array containing the active cell.
Ctrl+Shift+O	Select all cells that contain comments.
Ctrl+\	In a selected row, select the cells that don't match the value in the active cell.
Ctrl+Shift+|	In a selected column, select the cells that don't match the value in the active cell.
Ctrl+[	Select all cells directly referenced by formulas in the selection.

Ctrl+Shift+{	Select all cells directly or indirectly referenced by formulas in the selection.
Ctrl+]	Select cells that contain formulas that directly reference the active cell.
Ctrl+Shift+}	Select cells that contain formulas that directly or indirectly reference the active cell.
Alt+;	Select the visible cells in the current selection.

Extending a Selection

F8	Turn extend mode on or off. In extend mode, 'EXT' appears in the status line, and the arrow keys extend the selection.
Shift+F8	Add another range of cells to the selection; or use the arrow keys to move to the start of the range you want to add, and then press **F8** and the arrow keys to select the next range.
Shift+arrow	Extend the selection by one cell.
Ctrl+Shift+arrow	Extend the selection to the last nonblank cell in the same column or row.
Shift+Home	Extend the selection to the beginning of the row.
Ctrl+Shift+Home	Extend the selection to the beginning of the worksheet.
Ctrl+Shift+End	Extend the selection to the last used cell on the worksheet (lower-right corner).
Shift+Page Down	Extend the selection down one screen.
Shift+Page Up	Extend the selection up one screen.
End+Shift+arrow	Extend the selection to the last nonblank cell in the same column or row.
End+Shift+Home	Extend the selection to the last used cell on the worksheet (lower-right corner).

End+Shift+Enter   Extend the selection to the last cell in the current row.

Print Preview and Printing

Ctrl+P   Display the Print dialogue box.

In the Print Preview window the following shortcuts are active.

Arrow keys   Move around the page when zoomed in.
Page Up or Down   Move by one page when zoomed out.
Ctrl+ ⇑ or Ctrl+ ⇐   Move to the first page when zoomed out.
Ctrl+ ⇓ or Ctrl+ ⇒   Move to the last page when zoomed out.

Data Handling Shortcuts

Entering Data

Enter   Complete a cell entry and select the cell below.
Alt+Enter   Start a new line in the same cell.
Ctrl+Enter   Fill the selected cell range with the current entry.
Shift+Enter   Complete a cell entry and select the previous cell above.
Tab   Complete a cell entry and select the next cell to the right.
Shift+Tab   Complete a cell entry and select the previous cell to the left.
Esc   Cancel a cell entry.
⇑, ⇓, ⇐ or ⇒   Move one character up, down, left, or right.
Home   Move to the beginning of the line.
F4 or Ctrl+Y   Repeat the last action.

Ctrl+Shift+F3	Create names from row and column labels.
Ctrl+D	Fill down.
Ctrl+R	Fill to the right.
Ctrl+F3	Define a name.
Ctrl+K	Insert a hyperlink.
Ctrl+;	Enter the date.
Ctrl+Shift+:	Enter the time.
Alt+⇓	Display a drop-down list of the values in the current column of a range.
Ctrl+Z	Undo the last action.

Entering Special Characters

To enter special characters in a cell, press F2 to edit the cell, turn on Num Lock, and then press the following keys in the numeric key pad.

Alt+0162	Enters the cent character ¢.
Alt+0163	Enters the pound sterling character £.
Alt+0165	Enters the yen symbol ¥.
Alt+0128	Enters the euro symbol €.

Working with Formulas

=	Start a formula.
F2	Move the insertion point into the Formula Bar when editing in a cell is turned off.
Backspace	In the Formula Bar, delete one character to the left.
Enter	Complete a cell entry from the cell or Formula Bar.
Ctrl+Shift+Enter	Enter a formula as an array formula.
Esc	Cancel an entry in the cell or Formula Bar.

Shift+F3	In a formula, display the Insert Function dialogue box.
Ctrl+A	When the insertion point is to the right of a function name in a formula, display the Function Arguments dialogue box.
Ctrl+Shift+A	When the insertion point is to the right of a function name in a formula, insert the argument names and parentheses.
F3	Paste a defined name into a formula.
Alt+=	Insert an AutoSum formula with the **Sum** function.
Ctrl+Shift+"	Copy the value from the cell above the active cell into the cell or the Formula Bar.
Ctrl+'	Copies a formula from the cell above into the cell or the Formula Bar.
F9	Calculate all worksheets in all open workbooks. If a portion of a formula is selected, it calculates the portion.
Shift+F9	Calculate the active worksheet.
Ctrl+Alt+F9	Calculate all worksheets in all open workbooks, regardless of whether they have changed since the last calculation.
Ctrl+Alt+Shift+F9	Rechecks dependent formulas and then calculates all cells in all open workbooks, including cells not marked as needing to be calculated.

Editing Data

F2	Edit the active cell and position the insertion point at the end of the cell contents.
Alt+Enter	Start a new line in the same cell.
Backspace	Edit the active cell and then clear it, or delete the preceding character in the active cell as you edit cell contents.
Delete	Delete the character to the right of the insertion point, or delete the selection.

Ctrl+Delete	Delete text to the end of the line.
F7	Display the Spelling dialogue box.
Shift+F2	Edit a cell comment.
Enter	Complete a cell entry and select the next cell below.
Ctrl+Z	Undo the last action.
Esc	Cancel a cell entry.
Ctrl+Shift+Z	When the AutoCorrect Smart Tags is displayed, undo or redo the last automatic correction.

Manipulating Cells

Ctrl+C	Copy the selected cells.
Ctrl+C then Ctrl+C	Display the Microsoft Office Clipboard for multiple copy and paste operations.
Ctrl+X	Cut the selected cells.
Ctrl+V	Paste copied cells.
Delete	Clear the contents of the selected cells.
Ctrl+-	Delete the selected cells.
Ctrl+Shift+plus	Insert blank cells.

Formatting Data

Alt+'	Display the Style dialogue box.
Ctrl+1	Display the Format Cells dialogue box.
Ctrl+Shift+~	Apply the General number format.
Ctrl+Shift+$	Apply the Currency format with two decimal places and negative numbers in brackets.
Ctrl+Shift+%	Apply the Percentage format with no decimal places.
Ctrl+Shift+^	Apply the Exponential number format with two decimal places.

Ctrl+Shift+#	Apply the Date format with the day, month, and year.
Ctrl+Shift+@	Apply the Time format with the hour and minute, and AM or PM.
Ctrl+Shift+!	Apply the Number format with two decimal places, thousands separator, and minus sign (–) for negative values.
Ctrl+B	Apply or remove bold formatting.
Ctrl+I	Apply or remove italic formatting.
Ctrl+U	Apply or remove underlining.
Ctrl+5	Apply or remove strikethrough.
Ctrl+9	Hide the selected rows.
Ctrl+Shift+(	Unhide any hidden rows.
Ctrl+0	Hide the selected columns.
Ctrl+Shift+)	Unhide any hidden columns within the selection.
Ctrl+Shift+&	Apply the outline border.
Ctrl+Shift+_	Remove the outline border.

Using Borders

First press **Ctrl+1** to display the Format Cells dialogue box, and then use the Border tab.

Alt+T	Apply or remove the top border.
Alt+B	Apply or remove the bottom border.
Alt+L	Apply or remove the left border.
Alt+R	Apply or remove the right border.
Alt+H	If cells in multiple rows are selected, apply or remove the horizontal divider.
Alt+V	If cells in multiple columns are selected, apply or remove the vertical divider.
Alt+D	Apply or remove the downward diagonal border.
Alt+U	Apply or remove the upward diagonal border.

Handling Data Ranges

Using Data Forms

The following shortcuts can be used after actioning the **Data**, **Form** menu command.

⇩	Move to the same field in the next record.
⇧	Move to the same field in the previous record.
Tab and Shift+Tab	Move to each field in the record, then to each command button.
Enter	Move to the first field in the next record.
Shift+Enter	Move to the first field in the previous record.
Page Down	Move to the same field 10 records forward.
Ctrl+Page Down	Start a new, blank record.
Page Up	Move to the same field 10 records back.
Ctrl+Page Up	Move to the first record.
Home or End	Move to the beginning or end of a field.
Shift+End	Extend selection to the end of a field.
Shift+Home	Extend selection to the beginning of a field.
⇐ or ⇒	Move one character left or right within a field.
Shift+⇐	Select the character to the left within a field.
Shift+⇒	Select the character to the right within a field.

Using Filter Ranges

The following shortcuts can be used after actioning the **Data**, **AutoFilter** menu command.

Alt+⇓	In the cell that contains the drop-down arrow, displays the AutoFilter list for the current column.
⇓	Selects the next item in the AutoFilter list.
⇑	Selects the previous item in the AutoFilter list.
Alt+⇑	Closes the AutoFilter list for the current column.
Home	Selects the first item (All) in the AutoFilter list.
End	Selects the last item in the AutoFilter list.
Enter	Filters the range based on the item selected from the AutoFilter list.

Displaying Data Ranges

Alt+Shift+⇒	Groups rows or columns.
Alt+Shift+⇐	Ungroups rows or columns.
Ctrl+8	Displays or hides the outline symbols.
Ctrl+9	Hides the selected rows.
Ctrl+Shift+(	Unhides any hidden rows within the selection.
Ctrl+0	Hides the selected columns.
Ctrl+Shift+)	Unhides any hidden columns within the selection.

Chart Shortcuts

| F11 or Alt+F1 | Creates a chart of the data in the current range. |
| Ctrl+Page Down | Selects the next sheet in the workbook, until the chart sheet you want is selected. |

Ctrl+Page Up	Selects the previous sheet in the workbook, until the chart sheet you want is selected.
⇩	Select the previous group of elements in a chart.
⇧	Selects the next group of elements in a chart.
⇨	Selects the next element within a group.
⇦	Selects the previous element within a group.

Miscellaneous Shortcuts

When using speech recognition and text-to-speech

Ctrl	Switches between command mode and dictation mode.
Esc	Stops reading when text is being read aloud.

When sending e-mail messages as long as Microsoft Outlook is configured as your default e-mail program.

Shift+Tab	When cell A1 is selected, moves to the Introduction box in the e-mail message header.
	When in the message header, moves to the Subject, Bcc (if displayed), Cc, To, and From (if displayed) boxes, then to the address book for the Bcc, Cc, To, and From boxes, and then to cell A1.
Alt+S	Sends the e-mail message.
Ctrl+Shift+B	Opens the Address Book.
Alt+O	Opens the **Options** menu for access to the Options, Bcc Field, and From Field commands.

Alt+P	Opens the Outlook Message Options dialogue box.
Alt+K	Checks the names in the To, Cc, and Bcc boxes against the Address Book.
Alt+.	Opens the Address Book for the To box.
Alt+C	Opens the Address Book for the Cc box.
Alt+B	If the Bcc box is displayed, opens the Address Book for the Bcc box.
Alt+J	Goes to the Subject box.
Ctrl+Shift+G	Creates a message flag.
Alt+A	Adds interactivity to the range or sheet being sent.

Working with Macros

Alt+F8	Displays the Macro dialogue box.
Alt+F11	Displays the Visual Basic Editor.
Ctrl+F11	Inserts a Microsoft Excel 4.0 macro sheet.

Function Key Combinations

The following listings show many of the Excel keyboard shortcuts indexed by the use of the function keys.

F1	Displays the Help task pane.
F2	Edits the active cell and positions the insertion point at the end of the cell contents.
F3	Pastes a defined name into a formula.
F4	Repeats the last command or action, if possible.
F5	Displays the Go To dialogue box.
F6	Switches to the next pane in a worksheet that has been split.
F7	Displays the Spelling dialogue box to check spelling in the active worksheet or selected range.
F8	Turns extend mode on or off. In extend mode, EXT appears in the status line, and the arrow keys extend the selection.
F9	Calculates all worksheets in all open workbooks.
F9 then Enter	Calculates the selected portion of a formula and replaces it with the calculated value.
F10	Selects the menu bar or closes an open menu and submenu at the same time.
F11	Creates a chart of the data in the current range.
F12	Displays the Save As dialogue box.
Shift+F2	Edits a cell comment.
Shift+F3	Displays the Insert Function dialogue box.
Shift+F6	Switches to the previous pane in a worksheet that has been split.

Shift+F8	Enables you to add a non-adjacent cell or range to a selection of cells by using the arrow keys.
Shift+F9	Calculates the active worksheet.
Shift+F10	Displays the shortcut menu for a selected item.
Shift+F11	Inserts a new worksheet.
Ctrl+F1	Closes and reopens the current task pane.
Ctrl+F4	Closes the selected workbook window.
Ctrl+F5	Restores the window size of the selected workbook window.
Ctrl+F6	Switches to the next workbook window when more than one workbook window is open.
Ctrl+F7	Performs the Move command on the workbook window when it is not maximised. You can then use the arrow keys to move the window.
Ctrl+F8	Performs the **Size** command when a workbook is not maximised.
Ctrl+F9	Minimizes a workbook window to an icon.
Ctrl+F10	Maximises or restores the selected workbook window.
Alt+F1	Creates a chart of the data in the current range.
Alt+F8	Displays the Macro dialogue box to run, edit, or delete a macro.
Alt+F11	Opens the Visual Basic Editor for you to create a macro.
Alt+Shift+F1	Inserts a new worksheet.
Alt+Shift+F10	Displays the menu or message for a smart tag. If more than one smart tag is present, it switches to the next smart tag and displays its menu or message.

Alt+Shift+F11	Opens the Microsoft Script Editor, where you can add text, edit HTML tags, and modify any script code.
Ctrl+Alt+F9	Calculates all worksheets in all open workbooks, regardless of whether they have changed since the last calculation.
Ctrl+Alt+Shift+F9	Rechecks dependent formulas, and then calculates all cells in all open workbooks, including cells not marked as needing to be calculated.

Ctrl Key Combinations

The following listings show many of the Excel keyboard shortcuts indexed by the use of the **Ctrl** key.

Ctrl+(	Unhides any hidden rows within the selection.
Ctrl+)	Unhides any hidden columns within the selection.
Ctrl+&	Applies the outline border to the selected cells.
Ctrl+_	Removes the outline border from the selected cells.
Ctrl+~	Applies the General number format.
Ctrl+$	Applies the Currency format with two decimal places (negative numbers in parentheses).
Ctrl+%	Applies the Percentage format with no decimal places.
Ctrl+^	Applies the Exponential number format with two decimal places.
Ctrl+#	Applies the Date format with the day, month, and year.
Ctrl+@	Applies the Time format with the hour and minute, and AM or PM.
Ctrl+!	Applies the Number format with two decimal places, thousands separator, and minus sign (-) for negative values.
Ctrl+-	Displays the Delete dialogue box to delete the selected cells.
Ctrl+*	Selects the current region around the active cell.
Ctrl+:	Enters the current time.
Ctrl+;	Enters the current date.
Ctrl+`	Alternates between displaying cell values and displaying formulas in the worksheet.

Ctrl+'	Copies a formula from the cell above the active cell into the cell or the Formula Bar.
Ctrl+"	Copies the value from the cell above the active cell into the cell or the Formula Bar.
Ctrl+Plus	Displays the Insert dialogue box to insert blank cells.
Ctrl+1	Displays the Format Cells dialogue box.
Ctrl+2	Applies or removes bold formatting.
Ctrl+3	Applies or removes italic formatting.
Ctrl+4	Applies or removes underlining.
Ctrl+5	Applies or removes strikethrough.
Ctrl+6	Alternates between hiding objects, displaying objects, and displaying place-holders for objects.
Ctrl+7	Displays or hides the Standard toolbar.
Ctrl+8	Displays or hides the outline symbols.
Ctrl+9	Hides the selected rows.
Ctrl+0	Hides the selected columns.
Ctrl+A	Selects the entire worksheet.
Ctrl+Shift+A	Inserts the argument names and paren-theses when the insertion point is to the right of a function name in a formula.
Ctrl+B	Applies or removes bold formatting.
Ctrl+C	Copies the selected cells.
Ctrl+C then Ctrl+C	Displays the Microsoft Office Clipboard.
Ctrl+D	Uses the **Fill Down** command to copy the contents and format of the topmost cell of a selected range into the cells below.
Ctrl+F	Displays the Find dialogue box.
Ctrl+G	Displays the Go To dialogue box.
Ctrl+H	Displays the Find and Replace dialogue box.
Ctrl+I	Applies or removes italic formatting.

Ctrl+K	Displays the Insert Hyperlink dialogue box for new hyperlinks or the Edit Hyperlink dialogue box for selected existing hyperlinks.
Ctrl+L	Displays the Create List dialogue box.
Ctrl+N	Creates a new, blank file.
Ctrl+O	Displays the Open dialogue box to open or find a file.
Ctrl+Shift+O	Selects all cells that contain comments.
Ctrl+P	Displays the Print dialogue box.
Ctrl+R	Uses the **Fill Right** command to copy the contents and format of the leftmost cell of a selected range into the cells to the right.
Ctrl+S	Saves the active file with its current file name, location, and file format.
Ctrl+U	Applies or removes underlining.
Ctrl+V	Inserts the contents of the Clipboard at the insertion point and replaces any selection. Available only after you cut or copied an object, text, or cell contents.
Ctrl+W	Closes the selected workbook window.
Ctrl+X	Cuts the selected cells.
Ctrl+Y	Repeats the last command or action, if possible.
Ctrl+Z	Uses the **Undo** command to reverse the last command or to delete the last entry you typed.
Ctrl+Shift+Z	Uses the **Undo** or **Redo** command to reverse or restore the last automatic correction when AutoCorrect Smart Tags are displayed.

Other Useful Shortcut Keys

Arrows	Move one cell up, down, left, or right in a worksheet.
Ctrl+Arrow	Moves to the edge of the current data region in a worksheet.
Shift+Arrow	Extends the selection of cells by one cell.
Ctrl+Shift+Arrow	Extends the selection of cells to the last non-blank cell in the same column or row as the active cell.
⇐or ⇒	Selects the menu to the left or right when a menu is visible. When a submenu is open, these arrow keys switch between the main menu and the submenu.
⇓or ⇑	Selects the next or previous command when a menu or submenu is open.
Alt+ ⇓	Opens a selected drop-down list.
Backspace	Deletes one character to the left in the Formula Bar. It also clears the content of the active cell.
Delete	Removes the cell contents (data and formulas) from selected cells without affecting cell formats or comments.
	In cell editing mode, it deletes the character to the right of the insertion point.
End	Moves to the cell in the lower-right corner of the window when Scroll Lock is turned on.
Ctrl+End	Moves to the last cell on a worksheet, in the lowest used row of the rightmost used column.
Ctrl+Shift+End	Extends the selection of cells to the last used cell on the worksheet (the lower-right corner).
Enter	By default, completes a cell entry from the cell or the Formula Bar, and selects the cell below.

	In a data form, it moves to the first field in the next record.
	It opens a selected menu or performs the action for a selected command.
	In a dialogue box, it performs the action for the default command button in the box.
Alt+Enter	Starts a new line in the same cell.
Ctrl+Enter	Fills the selected cell range with the current entry.
Shift+Enter	Completes a cell entry and selects the cell above.
Esc	Cancels an entry in the cell, or Formula Bar. It also closes an open menu or submenu, dialogue box, or message window.
Home	Moves to the beginning of a row in a worksheet.
	Moves to the cell in the upper-left corner of the window when Scroll Lock is turned on.
	Selects the first command on the menu when a menu or submenu is visible.
Ctrl+Home	Moves to the beginning of a worksheet.
Ctrl+Shift+Home	Extends the selection of cells to the beginning of the worksheet.
Page Down	Moves one screen down in a worksheet.
Alt+Page Down	Moves one screen to the right in a worksheet.
Ctrl+Page Down	Moves to the next sheet in a workbook.
Page Up	Moves one screen up in a worksheet.
Alt+Page Up	Moves one screen to the left in a worksheet.
Ctrl+Page Up	Moves to the previous sheet in a workbook.

Space	In a dialogue box, performs the action for the selected button, or selects or clears a check box.
Ctrl+Space	Selects an entire column in a worksheet.
Shift+Space	Selects an entire row in a worksheet.
Ctrl+Shift+Space	Selects all objects on a worksheet when an object is selected.
Alt+Space	Displays the Control menu for the Excel window.
Tab	Moves one cell to the right in a worksheet.
	Moves between unlocked cells in a protected worksheet.
	Moves to the next option or option group in a dialogue box.
Shift+Tab	Moves to the previous cell in a worksheet or the previous option in a dialogue box.
Ctrl+Tab	Switches to the next tab in dialogue box.
Ctrl+Shift+Tab	Switches to the previous tab in a dialogue box.

If you would like more detail on actually using Excel 2003, then may we suggest you keep a lookout for our book BP544, *Microsoft Office 2003 explained*, also published by BERNARD BABANI (publishing) Ltd.

10

Microsoft Access 2003

Microsoft Access 2003 is a database management system (DBMS) designed to allow you to store, manipulate and retrieve information easily and quickly. A database is a collection of data that exists and is organised around a specific theme or requirement. It can be of the 'flat-file' type, or it can have relational capabilities, as in the case of Access, which is a relational database management system (RDBMS).

Access 2003 provides a powerful set of tools that are sophisticated enough for professional developers, yet 'easy to learn' for new users. With it you can create, or use, powerful database solutions that make organising, accessing, and sharing information relatively easy.

Access's Keyboard Shortcuts

Like the other applications in Office 2003, Access has an incredible number of keyboard shortcuts, most of which are listed in this chapter.

Don't forget that the general Office 2003 shortcuts listed in Chapter 6 are also usable from Access.

General Shortcuts

Ctrl+N	Open a new database.
Ctrl+O	Open an existing database.
Ctrl+P	Print the current or selected object.
S	Open the Page Setup dialogue box.
C or Esc	Cancel Print Preview or Layout Preview.
Ctrl+S	Save a database object.
F12 or Alt+F2	Open the Save As dialogue box.
F11	Bring the Database window to the front.
Ctrl+F6	Cycle between open windows.
Ctrl+F8	Turn on Resize mode for the active window (as long as it isn't maximised). You can then use the arrow keys to resize the window.
Alt+Space	Display the Control menu.
Shift+F10	Display the shortcut menu.
Ctrl+W or Ctrl+F4	Close the active window.
Alt+F11	Switch between the Visual Basic Editor and the previous active window.
Alt+Shift+F11	Switch to the Microsoft Script Editor from the previous active window.
F2	Display the complete hyperlink address for a selected hyperlink.
F7	Check spelling.
Shift+F2	Open the Zoom box to more easily enter data in small input areas.
Alt+Enter	Display a property sheet in Design view.
Alt+F4	Quit Microsoft Access, close a dialogue box, or close a property sheet.
Ctrl+F2	Invoke a Builder.
Ctrl+F11	Toggle between a custom menu bar and a built-in menu bar.
Ctrl+⇨	Toggle forward between views.
Ctrl+⇦	Toggle back between views.

Using a Combo Box

F4	Open a combo box.
F9	Refresh the contents of a Lookup field, list box or combo box.
⇓	Move down one line.
⇑	Move up one line.
Page Down	Move down one page.
Page Up	Move up one page.
Tab	Exit a combo box or list box.

Using Find and Replace

These only work when in Datasheet and Form views.

Ctrl+F	Open the Find tab in the Find and Replace dialogue box.
Ctrl+H	Open the Replace tab in the Find and Replace dialogue box.
Shift+F4	Find the next occurrence of the specified text when the Find and Replace dialogue box is closed.

Working in Design View

F2	Switch between Edit mode when the insertion point is displayed, and Navigation mode (when an entire field is selected and the insertion point is not visible). In Navigation mode, you can move between fields with the arrow keys.
F4	Switch to the property sheet.
F5	Switch to Form view.
F6	Switch between the upper and lower portions of a window.
F7	Switch to the Code Builder.
Shift+F7	Switch from the Visual Basic Editor to form or report Design view.

Editing Controls

These shortcuts work in form and report Design view.

Shift+Enter	Add a control to a section.
Ctrl+C	Copy selected control to the Clipboard.
Ctrl+X	Cut the selected control and copy it to the Clipboard.
Ctrl+V	Paste the contents of the Clipboard in the upper-left corner of the selected section.
Ctrl+⇒	Move the selected control to the right.
Ctrl+⇐	Move the selected control to the left.
Ctrl+⇧	Move the selected control up.
Ctrl+⇩	Move the selected control down.
Shift+⇩	Increase the height of the selected control.
Shift+⇒	Increase the width of the selected control.
Shift+⇧	Reduce the height of the selected control.
Shift+⇐	Reduce the width of the selected control.

Working with Wizards

Tab	Move to the **Help** button in the wizard.
Alt+N	Move to the next wizard window.
Alt+B	Move to the previous wizard window.
Alt+F	Close the wizard window.

Database Window Shortcuts

Working with Object Lists

F2	Rename a selected object.
⇓	Move down one line.
Page Down	Move down one window.
End	Move to the last object.
⇑	Move up one line.
Page Up	Move up one window.
Home	Move to the first object.
Ctrl+Tab	Cycle through the Objects bar top to bottom.
Shift+Ctrl+Tab	Cycle through the Objects bar bottom to top.
Enter or Alt+O	Open the selected table or query in Datasheet view, or the form in Form view.
Enter	Open the selected report in Print Preview.
Enter	Open the selected data access page in Page view.
Enter	Run the selected macro.
Ctrl+Enter	Open the selected table, query, form, report, data access page, macro, or module in Design view.
Alt+N	Create a new table, query, form, report, data access page, macro, or module.
F5	Refresh the Database window.
Ctrl+G	Display the Immediate window in the Visual Basic Editor.

Handling Text and Data

Selection Shortcuts

When selecting text in a field you can use the following shortcuts.

Shift+⇒	Extend the selection one character to the right.
Ctrl+Shift+⇒	Extend the selection one word to the right.
Shift+⇐	Extend the selection one character to the left.
Ctrl+Shift+⇐	Extend the selection one word to the left.

When selecting a field or record you can use the following shortcuts.

Tab	Select the next field.
F2	Switch between Edit mode and Navigation mode.
Shift+Space	Switch between selecting the current record and the first field of the current record, in Navigation mode.
Shift+⇑	Extend the selection to the previous record.
Shift+⇓	Extend the selection to the next record.
Ctrl+A	Select all records.

When extending a selection in Datasheet view you can use the following shortcuts.

F8	Turn on Extend mode (EXT appears in the lower-right corner of the window).
⇐ or ⇒	Extend a selection to adjacent fields.
⇑ or ⇓	Extend a selection to adjacent rows.
Shift+F8	Undo the previous extension.
Esc	Cancel Extend mode.

When selecting and moving a column in Datasheet view you can use the following shortcuts.

Ctrl+Space	Select the current column or cancel the column selection, in Navigation mode.
Shift+⇨	Select the column to the right.
Shift+⇦	Select the column to the left.
Ctrl+Shift+F8	Turn on Move mode in which you can move selected columns using ⇨or ⇦.

Editing Shortcuts

Don't forget that if the insertion point is not visible you can press F2 to display it.

When moving the insertion point in a field:

⇨	Move the insertion point one character to the right.
Ctrl+⇨	Move the insertion point one word to the right.
⇦	Move the insertion point one character to the left
Ctrl+⇦	Move the insertion point one word to the left.
End	Move the insertion point to the end of the field, in single-line fields.
Ctrl+End	Move the insertion point to the end of the field, in multiple-line fields.
Home	Move the insertion point to the beginning of the field, in single-line fields.
Ctrl+Home	Move the insertion point to the beginning of the field, in multiple-line fields.

When copying, moving, or deleting text:

Ctrl+C	Copy the selection to the Clipboard.

Ctrl+X	Cut the selection and copy it to the Clipboard.
Ctrl+V	Paste the contents of the Clipboard at the insertion point.
Backspace	Delete the selection, or the character, to the left of the insertion point.
Delete	Delete the selection or the character, to the right of the insertion point.
Ctrl+Delete	Delete all characters to the right of the insertion point.

When you want to undo changes you have made:

Ctrl+Z	Undo typing.
Esc	Undo changes in the current field or record.

When entering data in Datasheet or Form view:

Ctrl+;	Insert the current date.
Ctrl+Shift+:	Insert the current time.
Ctrl+Alt+Space	Insert the default value for a field.
Ctrl+'	Insert the value from the same field in the previous record.
Ctrl+Plus	Add a new record.
Ctrl+Minus	Delete the current record.
Shift+Enter	Save changes to the current record.
Space	Switch between the values in a check box or option button.
Ctrl+Enter	Insert a new line.

When refreshing fields with current data:

F9	Recalculate the fields in the window.
Shift+F9	Rerun a query so as to reflect changes to the records.

Navigating Records

Design View

F2	Switch between Edit mode (with insertion point displayed) and Navigation mode.
F4	Switch to the property sheet.
F5	Switch to Form view, when in form Design view.
F6	Switch between the upper and lower portions of a window.
F7	Switch to the Code Builder when in form or report Design view.
F8	Open the field list in a form, report , or data access page. If the field list is already open it moves the focus to it.
Shift+F7	Switch from the Visual Basic Editor to form or report Design view.
Shift+F7	Switch from a control's property sheet in form or report Design view to the design surface, without changing the focus.
Alt+Enter	Display a property sheet in Design view.
Enter or Alt+O	Open the selected form in Form view.
Ctrl+Enter	Open the selected table, query, form, report, data access page, macro, or module in Design view.
Ctrl+Tab	Moves the focus to a subsection.
Shift+Enter	Add a control to a section.
Ctrl+C	Copy the selected control to the Clipboard.
Ctrl+X	Cut the selected control and copy it to the Clipboard.
Ctrl+V	Paste the contents of the Clipboard in the upper-left corner of the selected section.
⇨ or ⇦	Move the selected control to the right or left by one pixel along the page grid.

⇧ or ⇩	Move the selected control up or down by one pixel along the page grid.
Ctrl+⇨ or ⇦	Move the selected control to the right or left by one pixel ignoring the page grid.
Ctrl+⇧ or ⇩	Move the selected control up or down by one pixel ignoring the page grid.
Shift+⇨ or ⇦	Increase or decrease the width of the selected control to the right or left by one pixel.
Shift+⇧ or ⇩	Decrease or increase the height of the selected control from the bottom or top by one pixel.
Esc	Move the focus from the Field List or Data Outline back to the data access page design surface.

Datasheet View

Some of these shortcuts will only work when you are in Navigation mode.

F5	Move to the record number box which displays the current record number in the lower-left corner. To move to another record, you can type its number in the box, and press Enter.
Tab or ⇨	Move to the next field.
End	Move to the last field in the current record.
Shift+Tab, or ⇦	Move to the previous field.
Home	Move to the first field in the current record.
⇩	Move to the current field in the next record.
Ctrl+⇩	Move to the current field in the last record.
Ctrl+End	Move to the last field in the last record.

⇧	Move to the current field in the previous record.
Ctrl+⇧	Move to the current field in the first record.
Ctrl+Home	Move to the first field in the first record.
Page Down	Go down one screen.
Page Up	Go up one screen.
Ctrl+Page Down	Go right one screen.
Ctrl+Page Up	Go left one screen.

Form View

F5	Move to the record number box which displays the current record number in the lower-left corner. To move to another record, you can type its number in the box, and press **Enter**.
Tab	Move to the next field.
Shift+Tab	Move to the previous field .
End	Move to the last field in the current record.
Ctrl+End	Move to the last field in the last record.
Home	Move to the first field in the current record.
Ctrl+Home	Move to the first field in the first record.
Ctrl+Page Down	Move to the current field in the next record.
Ctrl+Page Up	Move to the current field in the previous record.
Page Down	Go down one page. At the end of a record it moves to the equivalent page on the next record.
Page Up	Go up one page. At the end of a record it moves to the equivalent page on the previous record.

Print Preview and Layout Preview

P or Ctrl+P	Open the Print dialogue box.
S	Open the Page Setup dialogue box.
Z	Zoom in or out on a part of the page.
C or Esc	Cancel Print Preview or Layout Preview.
F5	Move to the page number box.
Page Down or ⇩	View the next page.
Page Up or ⇧	View the previous page.
⇩	Scroll down in small increments.
Page Down	Scroll down one full screen.
Ctrl+⇩	Move to the bottom of the page.
⇧	Scroll up in small increments.
Page Up	Scroll up one full screen.
Ctrl+⇧	Move to the top of the page.
⇨	Scroll to the right in small increments.
End or Ctrl+⇨	Move to the right edge of the page.
Ctrl+End	Move to the lower-right corner of the page.
⇦	Scroll to the left in small increments.
Home or Ctrl+⇦	Move to the left edge of the page.
Ctrl+Home	Move to the upper-left corner of the page.

PivotTable View

This is an Access view that summarises and analyses data in a datasheet or form.

F1	Display Help topics.
Shift+F10	Display the shortcut menu for the selected element of the PivotTable view.
Alt+Enter	Display the Properties dialogue box.
Alt+F4	Close the Properties dialogue box.
Ctrl+C	Copy the selected data from the Pivot-Table view to the Clipboard.

Ctrl+E	Export the contents of the PivotTable view to Microsoft Excel.
Ctrl+8	Show or hide the expand indicators (and boxes) beside items.
Ctrl+Plus	Expand the currently selected item.
Ctrl+Minus	Hide the currently selected item.
Alt+⇓	Open the list for the currently selected field.
Ctrl+T	Turn AutoFilter on or off.
Ctrl+Shift+A	Sort data in the selected field or total in ascending order.
Ctrl+Shift+Z	Sort data in the selected field or total in descending order.
Alt+Shift+⇑	Move the selected member up.
Alt+Shift+⇐	Move the selected member left.
Alt+Shift+⇓	Move the selected member down.
Alt+Shift+⇒	Move the selected member right.
Ctrl+L	Display or activate the field list.
⇑, ⇓, ⇐ or ⇒	Move to the next item in the field list.
Shift+⇑	Move to the previous item and include it in the selection.
Shift+⇓	Move to the next item and include it in the selection.
Ctrl+⇑	Move to the previous item, but do not include the item in the selection.
Ctrl+⇓	Move to the next item, but do not include the item in the selection.
Ctrl+Space	Remove the item from the selection.

To use these shortcut keys for formatting elements in PivotTable view, first select a detail field or a data cell for a total field.

Ctrl+Shift+~	Apply the general number format.
Ctrl+Shift+$	Apply the currency format, with two decimal places and negative numbers in parentheses.
Ctrl+Shift+%	Apply the percentage format, with no decimal places.
Ctrl+Shift+^	Apply the exponential number format, with two decimal places.
Ctrl+Shift+#	Apply the date format, with the day, month, and year
Ctrl+Shift+@	Apply the time format, with the hour, minute, and AM or PM.
Ctrl+Shift+!	Apply the numeric format, with two decimal places, thousands separator, and a minus sign for negative values.
Ctrl+B	Make selected text bold.
Ctrl+U	Make selected text underlined.
Ctrl+I	Make selected text italic.

If you would like more detail on actually using Access 2003, then may we suggest you keep a lookout for our book BP544, *Microsoft Office 2003 explained*, also published by BERNARD BABANI (publishing) Ltd.

11

Microsoft Publisher 2003

Microsoft Publisher is a desktop publishing program that allows you to quickly and easily create great-looking results that you can print on either your own printer, a commercial printer, or publish on the Web.

You can use Publisher to either design a publication from scratch with a variety of blank page templates whose margins and folds are already laid out for you, or use one of several Wizards that help you add your own contents to professionally designed templates under different categories. There are Wizards that help you create common types of publications, such as Newsletters, Brochures, Postcards, and Web sites, to mention but a few, with each type of publication offering different designs that you can choose from.

Publisher's Keyboard Shortcuts

Like the other applications in Office 2003, Publisher has an incredible number of keyboard shortcuts, most of which are listed in this chapter.

Don't forget that the general Office 2003 shortcuts listed in Chapter 6 are also usable in Publisher.

Editing and Formatting

Editing and Formatting Text

F3 or Ctrl+F	Display the Find and Replace task pane, with the Find option selected under Find or Replace.
Ctrl+H	Display the Find and Replace task pane, with the Replace option selected under Find or Replace.
F7	Check spelling.
Shift+F7	Display the Research task pane to find synonyms.
Ctrl+A	If there is an insertion point in a text box, this selects all the text in the current story. If there is no insertion point in any text box, it selects all the objects on a page.
Ctrl+B	Make text bold.
Ctrl+I	Italicise text.
Ctrl+U	Underline text.
Ctrl+Shift+K	Make text small capital letters, or return small capital letters to upper and lower case. (Not available in Web view).
Ctrl+Shift+S	Select the Style box on the Formatting toolbar.
Ctrl+Shift+F	Select the Font box on the Formatting toolbar.
Ctrl+Shift+P	Select the Font Size box on the Formatting toolbar.
Ctrl+Shift+C	Copy the formatting.
Ctrl+Shift+V	Paste formatting.
Ctrl+Shift+Y	Turn Special Characters on or off.
Ctrl+Space	Return character formatting to the current text style.
Ctrl+=	Apply or remove subscript formatting.

Ctrl+Shift+=	Apply or remove superscript formatting.
Ctrl+Shift+]	Increase kerning, or the space between letters in a word.
Ctrl+Shift+[	Decrease kerning.
Ctrl+]	Increase font size by 1.0 point.
Ctrl+[	Decrease font size by 1.0 point.
Ctrl+Shift+>	Increase to the next size in the Font Size box.
Ctrl+Shift+<	Decrease to the next size in the Font Size box.
Ctrl+E	Set centre alignment for a paragraph.
Ctrl+L	Set left alignment for a paragraph.
Ctrl+R	Set right alignment for a paragraph.
Ctrl+J	Set justified alignment for a paragraph.
Ctrl+Shift+H	Display the Hyphenation dialogue box. (Not available in Web view).
Alt+Shift+T	Insert the current time.
Alt+Shift+D	Insert the current date.
Alt+Shift+P	Insert the current page number.
Ctrl+Shift+0	Insert a zero-width non-breaking space.
Ctrl+1	Set the current paragraph to single spacing.
Ctrl+2	Set the current paragraph to double spacing.
Ctrl+5	Set the current paragraph to 1.5 line spacing.

Copying Text Formats

Ctrl+Shift+C	Copy formatting from text.
Ctrl+Shift+V	Apply copied formatting to text.

Manipulating Text and Objects

Ctrl+C	Copy the selected text or object.
Ctrl+X	Cut the selected text or object.
Ctrl+V	Paste text or an object.
Ctrl+Shift+X	Delete selected object.
Ctrl+Z	Undo the last action.
Ctrl+Y or F4	Redo the last action.
Esc	If text is selected, deselects the text, but the object that contains the text remains selected.
	If an object is selected, deselects the object.
	If an object within a group is selected, deselects the object but the group remains selected.
	If text within a grouped object is selected, selects the object within the group.
	If the Preview Gallery is open, closes it.
Arrow	Nudge a selected object up, down, left, or right.
Alt+Arrow	If the selected object has an insertion point in its text, nudges the selected object up, down, left, or right.
F9	Switch between the current view and the actual size.
Ctrl+Shift+L	Zoom to full page view.
Alt+F6	Bring layered object to the front.
Alt+Shift+F6	Send layered object to the back.
Ctrl+Shift+W	Turn **Snap to Guides** on or off.
Ctrl+A	Select all objects on the page.
Ctrl+Shift+G	Group or ungroup selected objects.
Ctrl+T	Switch between making an object transparent or opaque.
Ctrl+Shift+O	Turn **Boundaries and Guides** on or off.

Ctrl+F7	Turn **Horizontal Baseline Guides** on or off. (Not available in Web view).
Ctrl+Shift+F7	Turn **Vertical Baseline Guides** on or off. (Not available in Web view).

Working with Pages

If your publication is in two-page spread view, these commands will apply to the selected two-page spread. If not they will apply only to the selected page.

F5 or Ctrl+G	Display the Go To Page dialogue box.
Ctrl+Shift+N	Insert a page after the selected page.
Ctrl+Shift+U	Insert duplicate page after the selected page.
Ctrl+Page Down	Go to the next page.
Ctrl+Page Up	Go to the previous page.
Ctrl+M	Switch between the current page and the master page.

Working with Publications

Ctrl+N	Create a new blank publication.
Ctrl+O	Open a publication.
Ctrl+F4 or Ctrl+W	Close the current publication.
Ctrl+S	Save the current publication.

Using Print Preview

F9	Switch between the current view and the actual size.
⇧ or ⇩	Scroll up or down.
⇦ or ⇨	Scroll left or right .
Page or Ctrl+⇧	Scroll up in large increments.
Page or Ctrl+⇩	Scroll down in large increments.
Ctrl+⇦	Scroll left in large increments.
Ctrl+⇨	Scroll right in large increments.
Home	Scroll to the upper left corner of the page.
End	Scroll to the lower right corner of the page.
F5 or Ctrl+G	Display the Go To Page dialogue box.
Ctrl+Page Up	Go to the previous page.
Ctrl+Page Down	Go to the next page.
Ctrl+F6	Go to the next window.
Alt+F8	Display the Macros dialogue box.
Alt+F11	Display the Visual Basic editor.
Ctrl+P	Print the current publication.
Esc	Exit Print Preview.

Working with Web Pages

Ctrl+K	Insert a hyperlink at the insertion point in a text box.
Ctrl+Shift+B	Preview Web page.

Sending E-mail

After you have chosen **Send This Page as Message** or **Send Publication as Attachment** (from the **File** menu), you can use the following shortcut keys:

Alt+S	Send the current page or publication.
Ctrl+Shift+B	Open the Address Book, when the insertion point is in the message header.
Alt+K or Ctrl+K	When the insertion point is in the header, checks the names on the To, Cc, and Bcc lines against the Address Book.
Alt+.	Opens the Address Book in the To field, when the insertion point is in the message header.
Alt+C	Opens the Address Book in the Cc field.
Alt+B	If the Bcc field is visible, opens the Address Book in the Bcc field. To display the Bcc field, open the Address Book for any field and insert or type a name in the Bcc box.
Alt+J	Go to the Subject field.
Alt+P	Open the Microsoft Outlook Message Options dialogue box.
Ctrl+Shift+G	Create a message flag.
Tab	When the insertion point is in the message header, select the next box in the message header.
Shift+Tab	Select the previous field or button in the message header.
Ctrl+Tab	If the insertion point is in an object that contains text, and you then choose the **Send This Page as Message** or **Send Publication as Attachment** command from the **File** menu, the insertion point moves to the To field in the message header. You can then press **Ctrl+Tab** to select the Send button in the message header toolbar, and use the arrow keys

to move to the other buttons. To perform the action for the selected button or command, press **Enter**.

General Shortcuts

Alt+F8   Display the Macros dialogue box.

Alt+F11   Display the Visual Basic editor.

12

Microsoft PowerPoint 2003

Microsoft PowerPoint 2003 is a powerful and versatile Graphics Presentation package which deserves more attention than it gets from most users of Microsoft Office.

The key element of PowerPoint is the Slide Show and the production of ancillary material, such as scripted notes to accompany each slide, laser copies of slides, and an outline view of all the information in the presentation. However, Microsoft uses the word slide to refer to each individual page of a presentation and you can format the output for overhead projector acetates, or for electronic presentation on screen

PowerPoint's Keyboard Shortcuts

Like the other applications in Office 2003, PowerPoint has a large number of keyboard shortcuts, most of which are listed in this chapter.

Don't forget that the general Office 2003 shortcuts listed in Chapter 6 are also usable in PowerPoint.

Moving Between Panes

F6	Move clockwise among panes of normal view.
Shift+F6	Move anticlockwise among panes of normal view.
Ctrl+Shift+Tab	Switch between Slides and Outline tabs of the Outline and Slides pane in normal view.

Working in Outline

Alt+Shift+ ⇐	Promote a paragraph.
Alt+Shift+ ⇒	Demote a paragraph.
Alt+Shift+ ⇑	Move selected paragraphs up.
Alt+Shift+ ⇓	Move selected paragraphs down.
Alt+Shift+1	Show heading level 1.
Alt+Shift+Plus	Expand text below a heading.
Alt+Shift+Minus	Collapse text below a heading.
Alt+Shift+A	Show, or collapse, all text or headings.

Text and Objects

Shift+ ⇒	Select one character to the right.
Shift+ ⇐	Select one character to the left.
Ctrl+Shift+ ⇒	Select to the end of a word.
Ctrl+Shift+ ⇐	Select to the beginning of a word.
Shift+ ⇑	Select one line up.
Shift+ ⇓	Select one line down.
Esc	Select an object with text selected inside the object.
Enter	Select text within an object, when the object is selected.

Ctrl+A	Slides tab - Select all objects.
	Slide sorter view - Select all slides.
	Outline tab - Select all text.

Manipulating Text and Objects

Backspace	Delete one character to the left.
Ctrl+Backspace	Delete one word to the left.
Delete	Delete one character to the right.
Ctrl+Delete	Delete one word to the right.
Ctrl+X	Cut selected object to the Clipboard.
Ctrl+C	Copy selected object to the Clipboard.
Ctrl+V	Paste the cut or copied object.
Ctrl+Z	Undo the last action.

Navigating Text

⇐	Move one character to the left.
⇒	Move one character to the right.
⇑	Move one line up.
⇓	Move one line down.
Ctrl+⇐	Move one word to the left.
Ctrl+⇒	Move one word to the right.
End	Move to the end of a line.
Home	Move to the beginning of a line.
Ctrl+⇑	Move up one paragraph.
Ctrl+⇓	Move down one paragraph.
Ctrl+End	Move to the end of a text box.
Ctrl+Home	Move to the beginning of a text box.
Ctrl+Enter	Move to the next title or body text place-holder. If it is the last placeholder on a slide, this will insert a new slide with the same slide layout as the original.
Shift+F4	Repeat the last Find action.

Working in Tables

Tab	Move to the next cell.
Shift+Tab	Move to the preceding cell.
⇓	Move to the next row.
⇑	Move to the preceding row.
Ctrl+Tab	Insert a tab in a cell.
Enter	Start a new paragraph.

Formatting Text and Paragraphs

Ctrl+Shift+F	Change the font.
Ctrl+Shift+P	Change the font size.
Ctrl+Shift+>	Increase the font size.
Ctrl+Shift+<	Decrease the font size.
Ctrl+T	Change the case of characters between sentence, lowercase, and uppercase.
Shift+F3	Change the case of letters.
Ctrl+B	Apply bold formatting.
Ctrl+U	Apply an underline.
Ctrl+I	Apply italic formatting.
Ctrl+=	Apply subscript formatting.
Ctrl+Shift+Plus	Apply superscript formatting.
Ctrl+Space	Remove manual character formatting.
Ctrl+Shift+C	Copy formats.
Ctrl+Shift+V	Paste formats.
Ctrl+E	Centre paragraph.
Ctrl+J	Justify paragraph.
Ctrl+L	Left align paragraph.
Ctrl+R	Right align paragraph.

PowerPoint Presentations

Slide Shows

You can use the following shortcut keys when running PowerPoint slide show presentations in full-screen mode.

⇒, ⇓, N, Enter, Page Down, or Space	Perform the next animation or advance to the next slide.
⇐, ⇑, P, Page Up, or Backspace	Perform the previous animation or return to the previous slide.
F1	Show a list of available controls.
x+Enter	Go to slide number x.
B or .	Display a black screen, or return to the slide show from a black screen.
W or ,	Display a white screen, or return to the slide show from a white screen.
S or +	Stop or restart an automatic slide show.
Esc, Ctrl+Break	End a slide show.
E	Erase on-screen annotations.
H	Go to the next hidden slide.
T	Set new timings while rehearsing.
O	Use original timings while rehearsing.
M	Use mouse-click to advance while rehearsing.
1+Enter	Return to the first slide. You can also press both mouse buttons for 2 seconds.
Ctrl+P	Redisplay hidden pointer and/or change the pointer to a pen.
Ctrl+A	Redisplay hidden pointer and/or change the pointer to an arrow.
Ctrl+H	Hide the pointer and navigation button immediately.
Ctrl+U	Hide the pointer and navigation button in 15 seconds.

Shift+F10	Display the shortcut menu.
Tab	Go to the first or next hyperlink on a slide.
Shift+Tab	Go to the last or previous hyperlink on a slide.

Browsing Web Presentations

The following keys are for viewing your Web presentation in Internet Explorer 4.0, or later.

Tab	Move forward through the hyperlinks in a Web presentation, the Address bar, and the Links bar.
Shift+Tab	Move back through the hyperlinks in a Web presentation, the Address bar, and the Links bar.
Enter	Perform the mouse click behaviour of the selected hyperlink.
Space	Go to the next slide.
Backspace	Go to the previous slide.

Sending a Presentation by E-mail

When sending a presentation as the body of an e-mail message, you can use the following keys as long as the e-mail header is active. To activate the e-mail header, press Shift+Tab as many times as necessary.

Alt+S	Send as an e-mail message.
Ctrl+Shift+B	Open the Address Book.
Alt+K	Check the names on the To, Cc, and Bcc lines with the Address Book.
Tab	Select the next box in the e-mail header.
Shift+Tab	Select the previous field or button in the e-mail header.

13

Microsoft FrontPage 2003

FrontPage 2003 includes the professional design, authoring, data, and publishing tools needed for almost anybody to create dynamic and sophisticated Web sites.

Its enhanced design tools help produce better looking Web sites and make it easier to construct exactly the looks you want.

There are design tools to generate code faster, more efficiently, and with greater accuracy. Improved graphics support makes working with graphics from other applications very easy. Its professional coding tools, generate page code faster, more efficiently, and with greater accuracy.

FrontPage's Keyboard Shortcuts

Like the other applications in Office 2003, FrontPage has a large number of keyboard shortcuts, most of which are listed in this chapter. Be careful though, as some of them are only available in certain FrontPage views.

Also don't forget that the general Office 2003 shortcuts listed in Chapter 6 are also usable in FrontPage.

Managing Web Pages

F8	Run the accessibility checker.
Ctrl+N	Create a new Web page.
Ctrl+O	Open a Web page.
Ctrl+F4	Close a Web page.
Ctrl+S	Save a Web page.
Ctrl+P	Print a Web page.
F5	Refresh a Web page, or the Folder List.
Ctrl+Tab	Switch between open Web pages.
Ctrl+Shift+B	Preview a Web page in a Web browser.
Alt+F4	Quit Microsoft FrontPage.
Ctrl+Shift+8	Display nonprinting characters.
Ctrl+/	Display HTML tags in Design view.
Ctrl+F	Find text or HTML on a Web page.
Ctrl+H	Replace text or HTML on a Web page.
F7	Check spelling on a Web page.
Shift+F7	Look up a word in the Thesaurus.
Esc	Cancel an action.
Ctrl+Z	Undo an action.
Ctrl+Y	Redo or repeat an action.
Delete	Delete a Web page or folder in the Folder List or any dialogue box.
Backspace	Move up one level.

Different Views

F12	Preview the current page in a Web browser.
Ctrl+Page Up/Dn	Move between Code, Design, Split, and Preview views.

Alt+Page Up/Dn	Move between Code and Design panes in Split view.
Alt+F1	Show or hide the Folder List.
⇧, ⇩, ⇦ or ⇨	In Hyperlinks view, move through hyperlink nodes.
Shift+⇨	Expand the current node and move to the right in Hyperlinks view.
Shift+⇦	Expand the current node and move to the left in Hyperlinks view.

Working with Coding Tools

Ctrl+Q	Quick tag editor.
Ctrl+F2	Insert temporary bookmark.
F2	Go to next temporary bookmark.
Shift+F2	Go to previous temporary bookmark.
Ctrl+G	Go to line.
Ctrl+L	AutoComplete.
Ctrl+Enter	Insert code snippet.
Ctrl+>	Insert end tag.
Ctrl+<	Insert start tag.
Ctrl+/	Insert HTML comment.
Ctrl+Space	Complete word.

Formatting Shortcuts

Ctrl+Shift+F	Change the font.
Ctrl+Shift+P	Change the font size.
Ctrl+B	Apply bold formatting.
Ctrl+U	Apply an underline.
Ctrl+I	Apply italic formatting.
Shift+Tab	In the More Colors dialogue box, activate the color picker.
⇧, ⇩, ⇦ or ⇨	Use the color picker.
Ctrl+Plus	Apply superscript formatting.
Ctrl+Minus	Apply subscript formatting.
Ctrl+Shift+C	Copy formatting.
Ctrl+Shift+V	Paste formatting.
Ctrl+Space	Remove manual formatting.
Ctrl+E	Centre a paragraph.
Ctrl+L	Left align a paragraph.
Ctrl+R	Right align a paragraph.
Ctrl+M	Indent a paragraph from the left.
Ctrl+Shift+M	Indent a paragraph from the right.
Ctrl+Shift+S	Apply a style.
Ctrl+Shift+N	Apply the Normal style.
Ctrl+Alt+1	Apply the Heading 1 style.
Ctrl+Alt+2	Apply the Heading 2 style.
Ctrl+Alt+3	Apply the Heading 3 style.
Ctrl+Alt+4	Apply the Heading 4 style.
Ctrl+Alt+5	Apply the Heading 5 style.
Ctrl+Alt+6	Apply the Heading 6 style.
Ctrl+Shift+L	Apply the List style.

Text and Graphics

Backspace	Delete one character to the left.
Delete	Delete one character to the right.
Ctrl+Backspace	Delete one word to the left.
Ctrl+Delete	Delete one word to the right.
Ctrl+C	Copy text or graphics.
Ctrl+X	Cut selected text to the Office Clipboard.
Ctrl+V	Paste the Clipboard contents.
Shift+Enter	Insert a line break.
Ctrl+Shift+Space	Insert a nonbreaking space.
Shift+⇒	Select one character to the right.
Shift+⇐	Select one character to the left.
Ctrl+Shift+⇒	Select to the end of a word.
Ctrl+Shift +⇐	Select to the beginning of a word.
Shift+End	Select to the end of a line.
Shift+Home	Select to the beginning of a line.
Shift+⇑	Select one line up.
Shift+⇓	Select one line down.
Ctrl+Shift+⇓	Select to the end of a paragraph.
Ctrl+Shift+⇑	Select to the beginning of a paragraph.
Shift+Page Down	Select one screen down.
Shift+Page Up	Select one screen up.
Ctrl+A	Select the entire page.
Alt+Enter	Display the properties of a selection.

Tables, Graphics, and Hyperlinks

Shift+Ctrl+Alt+T	Insert a table.
Tab	Select the contents of the next table cell.
Shift+Tab	Select the contents of the preceding table cell.
Ctrl+T	Create an auto thumbnail of the selected graphic.
Ctrl+K	Create a hyperlink on a Web page.

14

Works Suite 2004 & Works 7.0

Microsoft Works Suite 2004 is a collection of powerful, fully featured, programs with a similar look and feel which, with the help of the Task Launcher, are made to work together as if they were a single program. The package was specifically designed for 'home use' to let you work with your data in an easily understood, but powerful, environment which enables you to quickly and efficiently obtain the results you want.

The core of Microsoft Works Suite 2004 is the Works 7.0 package which can be purchased as a separate, cheaper, entity. The main difference between the two packages is:

Works Suite 2004 has Microsoft Word 2002 as its word processor, not the slightly cut-down Works word processor that is included with the standard Works 7.0 package.

This book is designed to be useful for users of both packages, and as such, it includes keyboard shortcuts for the Works Task Launcher, the Works 7.0 word processor, and for the spreadsheet, database, calendar and address book tools common to both. Shortcuts for Word 2002 round off the chapter, many of which are similar to those for Word 2003 in Chapter 8, but are included for completeness.

The Works Task Launcher

The following keyboard shortcuts can be used to move the focus to the different tabs in the Task Launcher. You can then use the arrow keys on the keyboard to move through the choices within a tab.

⇐	Move one tab to the left.
⇒	Move one tab to the right.
Alt+O	Move to the Home page.
Alt+T	Move to the Templates page.
Alt+P	Move to the Programs page.
Alt+R	Move to the Project page.
Alt+S	Move to the History page.
Alt+A	Move to the Calendar tab on the Home page.
Alt+C	Move to the Contacts tab on the Home page.

After moving the focus to the Contacts tab, you can sort contact information using the following shortcuts:

Alt+N	Sort contacts by name.
Alt+E	Sort contacts by home phone number.
Alt+B	Sort contacts by business phone number.
Alt+M	Sort contacts by mobile phone number.
Alt+L	Sort contacts by E-mail address.

Works 7.0 Word Processor

The following keyboard shortcuts should help you use the program more easily and quickly.

⇑	Move insertion point up one line.
⇓	Move down one line.
Ctrl+End	Move to the end of document.
Ctrl+Home	Move to the beginning of document.
Page Up	Move up one screen.
Page Down	Move down one screen.
⇐	Move one character to the left.
⇒	Move one character to the right.
Ctrl+⇒	Move one word to the right.

Shift+⇑	Select one line up.
Shift+⇓	Select one line down.
Shift+Ctrl+End	Select to the end of document.
Shift+Ctrl+Home	Select to the beginning of document.
Shift+Page Up	Select up one screen.
Shift+Page Down	Select down one screen.
Shift+⇐	Select one character to the left.
Shift+⇒	Select one character to the right.
Shift+Ctrl+⇒	Select one word to the right.

F1	Display Help for the program.
F7	Check spelling and grammar.
Shift+F7	Open the Thesaurus to find synonyms for selected word.
Ctrl+N	Display the Works Task Launcher to open a new document.
Ctrl+O	Open an existing document.
Ctrl+W	Close current document.
Ctrl+S	Save current document to disc.
Ctrl+P	Print current document.

Ctrl+C	Copy text to clipboard.
Ctrl+X	Cut text to clipboard.
Ctrl+V	Paste text from clipboard.
Ctrl+Z	Undo last action.
Ctrl+Y	Reverse last Undo action.
Del	Delete current selection.
Ctrl+A	Select an entire document.
Ctrl+F	Find specified text in document.
Ctrl+H	Finds and replaces specified text.
Ctrl+G	Go to specified item.
Ctrl+Enter	Insert hard page break.
Ctrl+1	Single line spacing.
Ctrl+5	Add 1½ spacing between text.
Ctrl+2	Double-space text.
Ctrl+3	Triple-space text.
Ctrl+B	Make text bold.
Ctrl+U	Underline text.
Shift+Ctrl+W	Underline text, but not the spaces between.
Ctrl+I	Make text italic.
Alt+O+P	Open the Format Paragraph dialogue box.
Ctrl+E	Centre align a paragraph.
Ctrl+J	Justify a paragraph.
Ctrl+L	Left align a paragraph.
Ctrl+R	Right align a paragraph.
Ctrl+M	Indent a paragraph from the left.
Ctrl+Shift+M	Remove a paragraph indent from the left.
Ctrl+T	Create a hanging indent.
Shift+Ctrl+T	Remove a hanging indent.
Ctrl+Q	Remove paragraph formatting.

Works 7.0 Spreadsheet

⇧	Move up one row.
⇩	Move down one row.
Ctrl+End	Move to the end of a cell when in Edit mode (entered by pressing **F2**).
Ctrl+Home	Move to the beginning of a cell when in Edit mode (**F2**).
Page Up	Move up one screen.
Page Down	Move down one screen.
⇐	Move one character to the left when in Edit mode (**F2**).
⇒	Move one character to the right when in Edit mode (**F2**).
⇐	Move one cell to the left when **not** in Edit mode.
⇒	Move one cell to the right when **not** in Edit mode.
Ctrl+⇐	Move one word to the left when in Edit mode (**F2**).
Ctrl+⇒	Move one word to the right when in Edit mode (**F2**).
Ctrl+⇧	Move to the beginning of a column when there are values in every cell in the column. If empty cells separate groups of values, move to the beginning of each group of values.
Ctrl+⇩	Move to the end of a column when there are values in every cell in the column. If empty cells separate groups of values, move to the end of each group of values.
Ctrl+N	Display the Works Task Launcher to open a new document.
Ctrl+O	Open an existing document.
Ctrl+W	Close current document.

Ctrl+S	Save current document to disc.
Ctrl+P	Print current document.
Ctrl+C	Copy text to clipboard.
Ctrl+X	Cut text to clipboard.
Ctrl+V	Paste text from clipboard.
Del	Clear the current selection.
Ctrl+A	Select the entire document.
Ctrl+F	Select next occurrence of specified text in document.
Ctrl+H	Select and replace next occurrence of specified text in document.
Ctrl+G	Go to and select specified cell, or range.
Ctrl+D	Fill down - Copies topmost cell(s) to the rest of the selection.
Ctrl+R	Fill right - Copies leftmost cell(s) to the rest of the selection.
Ctrl+Y	Apply repeat formatting to the selection.
F1	Display Help for the program.
F2	Invokes Edit mode.
F7	Check document for incorrect spelling.
F9	Recalculate spreadsheet or cell, when Manual Calculation is switched on.

Works 7.0 Database

⇑	Move up one row.
⇓	Move down one row.
Ctrl+End	Move to the end of a field when in Edit mode (entered by pressing **F2**).
Ctrl+Home	Move to the beginning of a field when in Edit mode (**F2**).
Page Up	Move up one screen.
Page Down	Move down one screen.
⇐	Move one character to the left when in Edit mode (**F2**).
⇒	Move one character to the right when in Edit mode (**F2**).
⇐	Move one cell to the left when **not** in Edit mode.
⇒	Move one cell to the right when **not** in Edit mode.
Ctrl+ ⇐	Move one word to the left when in Edit mode (**F2**).
Ctrl+ ⇒	Move one word to the right when in Edit mode (**F2**).
Ctrl+ ⇑	Move to the beginning of a column in the Database when there are values in every cell in the column. If empty cells separate groups of values, move to the beginning of each group of values.
Ctrl+ ⇓	Move to the end of a column in the Database when there are values in every cell in the column. If empty cells separate groups of values, move to the end of each group of values.
Ctrl+N	Display the Works Task Launcher to open a new document.
Ctrl+O	Open an existing document.

Ctrl+W	Close current document.
Ctrl+S	Save current document to disc.
Ctrl+P	Print current document.
Ctrl+C	Copy text to clipboard.
Ctrl+X	Cut text to clipboard.
Ctrl+V	Paste text from clipboard.
Ctrl+Shift+X	Cut database record.
Ctrl+Shift+C	Copy database record.
Ctrl+F	Select next occurrence of specified text in document.
Ctrl+G	Go to and select specified record, or field.
F1	Display Help for the program.
F2	Invokes Edit mode.
F7	Check document for incorrect spelling.
F9	Display Form view.
Shift+F9	Display List view.
Ctrl+F9	Display Form Design view in which you can change or move field names, labels or objects.

Works 7.0 Calendar

You can use the following keyboard shortcuts to move through the Works Calendar. Their actions depend on which Calendar view you are using.

Day in Hours View

⇧	Move up one half hour.
⇩	Move down one half hour.
⇦ or ⇨	Open an appointment for editing.
Tab	Move forward from appointment to appointment.
Shift+Tab	Move backward from appointment to appointment.
Page Up	Move backward through the day.
Page Down	Move forward through the day.
Esc	Move out of opened appointment without saving changes.
Ctrl+Tab	Cycle between Appointments, Help window, and Categories, when these areas are open.

Day View

⇧	Move up one appointment.
⇩	Move down one appointment.
Tab	Move forward from appointment to appointment.
Shift+Tab	Move backward from appointment to appointment.
Page Up	Move backward through the day.
Page Down	Move forward through the day.
Esc	Move out of opened appointment without saving changes.
Ctrl+Tab	Cycle between Appointments, Help window, and Categories, when these areas are open.

Week View

⇧	Move up one day.
⇩	Move down one day.
Tab	Move forward from appointment to appointment.
Shift+Tab	Move backward from appointment to appointment.
Page Up	Move backward through the day.
Page Down	Move forward through the day.
Esc	Move out of opened appointment without saving changes.
Ctrl+Tab	Cycle between Appointments, Help window, and Categories, when these areas are open.

Month View

⇐	Move one day to the left.
⇒	Move one day to the right.
⇧	Move up one week.
⇩	Move down one week.
Page Up	Move up one month.
Page Down	Move down one month.
Tab	Move forward from item to item, and open that item.
Shift+Tab	Move backward from item to item, and open that item.
Esc	Move out of opened appointment without saving changes.
Ctrl+Tab	Cycle between Appointments, Help window, and Categories, when these areas are open.

General Shortcuts

Ctrl+N	Create a new appointment.
Ctrl+O	Edit the selected appointment.
Ctrl+P	Set print options and print document.
Ctrl+F	Search Calendar for the specified type of appointment.
Alt+1	Show Calendar one day at a time.
Alt+-	Show Calendar one week at a time.
Alt+=	Show Calendar one month at a time.
F1	Display Help for the program.

Works 7.0 Address Book

The following few keyboard shortcuts work specifically with the Address Book of Works 7.0.

Ctrl+N	Create a new contact.
Ctrl+G	Create a new group.
Ctrl+R	Create a new folder.
Ctrl+P	Print information from the Address Book.
Ctrl+C	Copy selected entry.
Ctrl+V	Paste selected entry from the clipboard.
Ctrl+A	Select all Address Book entries.
Ctrl+F	Search for people on Internet directory services.
Alt+Enter	Edit the properties of the selected entries.
F1	Display Address Book Help.
F5	Refresh displayed information.

Word 2002 Shortcuts

Works Suite 2004 has Microsoft Word 2002 as its word processor, so we cover here most of its extensive list of keyboard shortcuts. The available function key combinations are shown at the end.

Quick Reference

Keyboard shortcuts for some of the most common tasks done in a Microsoft Word document are:

Ctrl+Shift+Space	Create a nonbreaking space.
Ctrl+-	Create a nonbreaking hyphen.
Ctrl+B	Make letters bold.
Ctrl+I	Make letters italic.
Ctrl+U	Make letters underline.
Ctrl+Shift+<	Decrease font size.
Ctrl+Shift+>	Increase font size.
Ctrl+Space	Remove formatting.
Ctrl+C	Copy the selected text or object.
Ctrl+X	Cut the selected text or object.
Ctrl+V	Paste text or an object.
Ctrl+Z	Undo the last action.
Ctrl+Y	Redo the last action.

Working with Documents

Ctrl+N	Create a new document of the same type as the current or most recent one.
Ctrl+O	Open a document.
Ctrl+W	Close a document.
Alt+Ctrl+S	Split the document window.
Alt+Shift+C	Remove the document window split.
Ctrl+S	Save a document.

Ctrl+F	Find text, formatting, and special items.
Alt+Ctrl+Y	Repeat find operation.
Ctrl+H	Replace text, specific formatting, and special items.
Ctrl+G	Go to a page, bookmark, footnote, table, comment, graphic, or other location.
Alt+Ctrl+Z	Go back to a page, bookmark, footnote, table, comment, graphic, or other location.
Alt+Ctrl+Home	Browse through a document.
Esc	Cancel an action.
Ctrl+Z	Undo an action.
Ctrl+Y	Redo or repeat an action.
Alt+Ctrl+P	Switch to print layout view.
Alt+Ctrl+O	Switch to outline view.
Alt+Ctrl+N	Switch to normal view.
Ctrl+\	Move between a master document and its subdocuments.
Alt+Shift+O	Mark a table of contents entry.
Alt+Shift+I	Mark a table of authorities entry.
Alt+Shift+X	Mark an index entry.
Alt+Ctrl+F	Insert a footnote.
Alt+Ctrl+D	Insert an endnote.

Printing and Previewing Documents

Ctrl+P	Print a document.
Alt+Ctrl+I	Switch in or out of print preview mode.
⇑, ⇓, ⇐ or ⇒	Move around the preview page when zoomed in.
Page Up / Down	Move by one preview page when zoomed out.
Ctrl+Home	Move to the first preview page when zoomed out.
Ctrl+End	Move to the last preview page when zoomed out.

Reviewing Documents

Alt+Ctrl+M	Insert a comment.
Ctrl+Shift+E	Turn 'track changes' on or off.
Alt+Shift+C	Close the Reviewing Pane if it is open.

Working with Text and Graphics

Backspace	Delete one character to the left.
Ctrl+Backspace	Delete one word to the left.
Delete	Delete one character to the right.
Ctrl+Delete	Delete one word to the right.
Ctrl+X	Cut selected text to the Clipboard.
Ctrl+Z	Undo the last action.
Ctrl+F3	Cut to the Spike.
Ctrl+C	Copy text or graphics to the Clipboard.
Ctrl+C, Ctrl+C	Display the Office Clipboard.
Alt+F3	Create AutoText.
Ctrl+V	Paste the Clipboard contents.
Ctrl+Shift+F3	Paste the Spike.
Alt+Shift+R	Copy the header or footer used in the previous section of the document.

Moving Around a Document

⇐	Move one character to the left.
⇒	Move one character to the right.
Ctrl+⇐	Move one word to the left.
Ctrl+⇒	Move one word to the right.
Ctrl+⇑	Move one paragraph up.
Ctrl+⇓	Move one paragraph down.
Shift+Tab	Move one cell to the left in a table.
Tab	Move one cell to the right in a table.
⇑	Move up one line.

⇓	Move down one line.
End	Move to the end of a line.
Home	Move to the beginning of a line.
Alt+Ctrl+Page Up	Move to the top of the window.
Alt+Ctrl+Page Dn	Move to the end of the window.
Page Up	Move up one screen.
Page Down	Move down one screen.
Ctrl+Page Dn	Move to the top of the next page.
Ctrl+Page Up	Move to the top of the previous page.
Ctrl+End	Move to the end of a document.
Ctrl+Home	Move to the beginning of a document.
Shift+F5	Move to a previous revision.
Shift+F5	Move to the location of the insertion point when the document was last closed.

Selecting Text and Graphics

As in most Windows applications you select text by holding down the **Shift** key and pressing the key that moves the insertion point. In Word you can also select multiple non-contiguous areas (ones that aren't next to each other) by holding down the **Ctrl** key and making the other selections you want. To extend a selection:

F8	Turn extend mode on.
F8, ⇐ or ⇒	Select the nearest character.
F8, F8...	Increase the size of a selection. Press once to select a word, twice to select a sentence, etc.
Shift+F8	Reduce the size of a selection.
Esc	Turn extend mode off.
Shift+⇒	Select one character to the right.
Shift+⇐	Select one character to the left.
Ctrl+Shift+⇒	Select to the end of a word.
Ctrl+Shift+⇐	Select to the beginning of a word.
Shift+End	Select to the end of a line.

Shift+Home	Select to the beginning of a line.
Shift+⇩	Select one line down.
Shift+⇧	Select one line up.
Ctrl+Shift+⇩	Select to the end of a paragraph.
Ctrl+Shift+⇧	Select to the beginning of a paragraph.
Shift+Page Down	Select one screen down.
Shift+Page Up	Select one screen up.
Ctrl+Shift+Home	Select to the beginning of a document.
Ctrl+Shift+End	Select to the end of a document.
Ctrl+A	Select the entire document.
Ctrl+Shift+F8	Select a vertical block of text with the arrow keys. Pressing **Esc** cancels this selection mode.
Alt+drag	Select a vertical column of text.

Characters and Formatting

Ctrl+F9	Insert a field.
Shift+Enter	Insert a line break.
Ctrl+Enter	Insert a page break.
Ctrl+Shift+Enter	Insert a column break.
Ctrl+Minus	Insert an optional hyphen.
Ctrl+Shift+Minus	Insert a nonbreaking hyphen.
Ctrl+Shift+Space	Insert a nonbreaking space.
Alt+Ctrl+C	Insert the copyright symbol ©.
Alt+Ctrl+R	Insert the registered trademark symbol ®.
Alt+Ctrl+T	Insert the trademark symbol '™'.
Alt+Ctrl+period	Insert an ellipsis '…'.
Ctrl+Shift+C	Copy formatting from text.
Ctrl+Shift+V	Apply copied formatting to text.
Ctrl+Shift+F	Change the font.
Ctrl+Shift+P	Change the font size.
Ctrl+Shift+>	Increase the font size.
Ctrl+Shift+<	Decrease the font size.

Ctrl+]	Increase the font size by 1 point.
Ctrl+[	Decrease the font size by 1 point.
Ctrl+D	Change the formatting of characters in the Font dialogue box.
Shift+F3	Change the case of letters.
Ctrl+Shift+A	Format letters as all capitals.
Ctrl+B	Apply bold formatting.
Ctrl+U	Underline all of selection.
Ctrl+Shift+W	Underline selected words but not spaces.
Ctrl+Shift+D	Double-underline text.
Ctrl+Shift+H	Apply hidden text formatting.
Ctrl+I	Apply italic formatting.
Ctrl+Shift+K	Format letters as small capitals.
Ctrl+=	Apply subscript formatting.
Ctrl+Shift+Plus	Apply superscript formatting.
Ctrl+Space	Remove manual character formatting.
Ctrl+Shift+Q	Change the selection to the Symbol font.
Ctrl+Shift+*	Display nonprinting characters.
Shift+F1	Review text formatting.
Ctrl+Shift+C	Copy formats.
Ctrl+Shift+V	Paste formats.
Ctrl+1	Single-space lines.
Ctrl+2	Double-space lines.
Ctrl+5	Set 1.5-line spacing.
Ctrl+0	Add or remove one line space preceding a paragraph.
Ctrl+E	Centre justify a paragraph.
Ctrl+J	Justify a paragraph.
Ctrl+L	Left align a paragraph.
Ctrl+R	Right align a paragraph.
Ctrl+M	Indent a paragraph from the left.
Ctrl+Shift+M	Remove a paragraph indent from the left.
Ctrl+T	Create a hanging indent.
Ctrl+Shift+T	Reduce a hanging indent.

Ctrl+Q	Remove paragraph formatting.
Ctrl+Shift+S	Apply a style.
Alt+Ctrl+K	Start AutoFormat.
Ctrl+Shift+N	Apply the Normal style.
Alt+Ctrl+1	Apply the Heading 1 style.
Alt+Ctrl+2	Apply the Heading 2 style.
Alt+Ctrl+3	Apply the Heading 3 style.
Ctrl+Shift+L	Apply the List style.

Outline View

Alt+Ctrl+O	Switch to outline view.
Alt+Shift+⇐	Promote a paragraph.
Alt+Shift+⇒	Demote a paragraph.
Ctrl+Shift+N	Demote to body text.
Alt+Shift+⇑	Move selected paragraphs up.
Alt+Shift+⇓	Move selected paragraphs down.
Alt+Shift+Plus	Expand text under a heading.
Alt+Shift+Minus	Collapse text under a heading.
Alt+Shift+A	Expand or collapse all text or headings.
/	Hide or display character formatting.
Alt+Shift+L	Show the first line of body text or all body text.
Alt+Shift+1	Show all headings with the Heading 1 style.
Alt+Shift+n	Show all headings up to Heading n
Ctrl+Tab	Insert a tab character.

Using Mail Merge

Alt+Shift+K	Preview a mail merge.
Alt+Shift+N	Merge a document.
Alt+Shift+M	Print the merged document.

Alt+Shift+E	Edit a mail-merge data document.
Alt+Shift+F	Insert a merge field.
Alt+Shift+D	Insert a DATE field.
Alt+Ctrl+L	Insert a LISTNUM field.
Alt+Shift+P	Insert a PAGE field.
Alt+Shift+T	Insert a TIME field.
Ctrl+F9	Insert an empty field.
Ctrl+Shift+F7	Update linked information in a Microsoft Word source document.
F9	Update selected fields.
Ctrl+Shift+F9	Unlink a field.
Shift+F9	Switch between a selected field code and its result.
Alt+F9	Switch between all field codes and their results.
Alt+Shift+F9	Run GOTOBUTTON or MACROBUTTON from the field that displays the field results.
F11	Go to the next field.
Shift+F11	Go to the previous field.
Ctrl+F11	Lock a field.
Ctrl+Shift+F11	Unlock a field.

Working in Tables

Tab	Move to and select the next cell in a row.
Shift+Tab	Move to and select the previous cell in a row.
Alt+Home	Move to the first cell in a row.
Alt+End	Move to the last cell in a row.
Alt+Page Up	Move to the first cell in a column.
Alt+Page Down	Move to the last cell in a column.
⇑	Move to the previous row.
⇓	Move to the next row.

Alt+5	Select an entire table. Use the numeric keypad with **Num Lock** off.
Enter	Insert a new paragraph in a cell.
Ctrl+Tab	Insert a tab character in a cell.

Working with Web Pages

To use the following shortcuts to go back or forward one page or to refresh a page, the Web toolbar must be showing. If not, press **Alt+V**, press **T**, use the arrow keys to select Web, and then press **Enter**.

Ctrl+K	Insert a hyperlink .
Alt+ ⇐	Go back one page.
Alt+ ⇒	Go forward one page.
F9	Refresh.

Using Word for E-mails

Many of the following shortcuts need you to activate the e-mail header, by pressing **Shift+Tab**.

Alt+S	Send the active document or message.
Ctrl+Shift+B	Open the Address Book.
Alt+K, Ctrl+K	When the insertion point is in the message header, check the names on the To, Cc, and Bcc lines against the Address Book.
Alt+.	Open the Address Book in the To field.
Alt+C	When the insertion point is in the message header, open the Address Book in the Cc field.
Alt+B	If the Bcc field is visible, open the Address Book in the Bcc field. To display the Bcc field, open the Address Book for any field and type a name in the Bcc box.
Alt+J	Go to the Subject field.

Alt+P	Open the Microsoft Outlook Message Options dialogue box.
Ctrl+Shift+G	Create a message flag.
Tab	When the insertion point is in the message header, select the next box in the e-mail header, or the body of the message.
Shift+Tab	Select the previous field or button in the e-mail header.
Ctrl+Tab	When the insertion point is in the message header, select the **Send** button.

Function Key Combinations

F1	Get Help or the Office Assistant.
F2	Move text or graphics.
F3	Insert an AutoText entry.
F4	Repeat the last action.
F5	Choose the **Go To** command.
F6	Go to the next pane or frame.
F7	Choose the **Spelling** command.
F8	Extend a selection.
F9	Update selected fields.
F10	Activate the menu bar.
F11	Go to the next field.
F12	Choose the **Save As** command.
Shift+F1	Start context-sensitive Help or reveal formatting.
Shift+F2	Copy text.
Shift+F3	Change the case of letters.
Shift+F4	Repeat a Find or Go To action.
Shift+F5	Move to the last change.
Shift+F6	Go to the previous pane or frame.
Shift+F7	Open the Thesaurus.

Shift+F8	Shrink a selection.
Shift+F9	Switch between a field code and its result.
Shift+F10	Display a shortcut (or control) menu.
Shift+F11	Go to the previous field.
Shift+F12	Choose the **Save** command.
Ctrl+F2	Choose the **Print Preview** command.
Ctrl+F3	Cut to the Spike (A special AutoText entry that stores multiple deletions).
Ctrl+F4	Close the window.
Ctrl+F5	Restore the document window size.
Ctrl+F6	Go to the next window.
Ctrl+F7	Choose the **Move** command.
Ctrl+F8	Choose the **Size** command.
Ctrl+F9	Insert an empty field.
Ctrl+F10	Maximise the document window.
Ctrl+F11	Lock a field.
Ctrl+F12	Choose the **Open** command.
Ctrl+Shift+F3	Insert the contents of the Spike.
Ctrl+Shift+F5	Edit a bookmark.
Ctrl+Shift+F6	Go to the previous window.
Ctrl+Shift+F7	Update linked information in a Microsoft Word source document.
Ctrl+Shift+F8	Extend a selection or block by then pressing an arrow key.
Ctrl+Shift+F9	Unlink a field.
Ctrl+Shift+F10	Activate the ruler.
Ctrl+Shift+F11	Unlock a field.
Ctrl+Shift+F12	Choose the **Print** command.
Alt+F1	Go to the next field.
Alt+F3	Create an AutoText entry.
Alt+F4	Quit Microsoft Word.
Alt+F5	Restore the program window size.

Alt+F7	Find the next misspelling or grammatical error, as long as the **Check spelling as you type** check box is selected in the **Spelling & Grammar** tab of the **Tools**, **Options** dialogue box.
Alt+F8	Run a macro.
Alt+F9	Switch between all field codes and their results.
Alt+F10	Maximise the program window.
Alt+F11	Display Microsoft Visual Basic code.
Alt+Shift+F1	Go to the previous field.
Alt+Shift+F2	Choose the **Save** command.
Alt+Shift+F9	Run GOTOBUTTON or MACROBUTTON from the field that displays the field results.
Alt+Shift+F11	Display Microsoft Visual Studio code.
Ctrl+Alt+F1	Display Microsoft System Information.
Ctrl+Alt+F2	Choose the **Open** command.

If you would like more detail on actually using Works Suite 2004 or Works 7.0, then may we suggest you keep a lookout for our book BP546, *Microsoft Works Suite 2004 explained*, also published by BERNARD BABANI (publishing) Ltd.

15

Paint Shop Pro 8

Paint Shop Pro 8, is part of the Paint Shop family of digital imaging and photography products produced by Jasc Software. They describe it as "the most complete, easy-to-use software for creating professional digital imaging results. By combining automatic and precision tools with an integrated learning system, Paint Shop Pro helps you produce professional results with power and ease".

You can use Paint Shop Pro to create and edit electronic paintings or almost any other type of graphic image. Perhaps most people these days use it to handle and edit their digital camera images, or to design and create graphics for Web pages or other presentations.

Like most graphics programs Paint Shop Pro is quite complex and has very extensive menu bars, tool bars and palettes. The following is a list of PSP's keyboard shortcuts, many require you to press two keys. For example, **Ctrl+A** means hold down the **Ctrl** key and press the letter **A**.

File Menu

Ctrl+B	Browse through images on disc.
Ctrl+F4	Close this image.
Ctrl+Delete	Delete this image file from the disc.
Ctrl+N	Create new image.
Ctrl+O	Open an existing document.
Ctrl+P	Print the active document.
Ctrl+S	Save the active document.
F12	Save the active document with a new name.
Ctrl+F12	Save a copy of the active document with a new name.
Shift+Alt+D	Deletes a previously saved workspace.
Shift+Alt+L	Loads the current workspace.
Shift+Alt+S	Saves the current workspace.

Edit Menu

Delete	Clear the selection or image.
Ctrl+Shift+Z	Show the command history for the current document.
Ctrl+C; Ctrl+Insert	Copy the selection from the current layer into the clipboard.
Ctrl+Shift+C	Copy the current merged image.
Ctrl+X	Cut out the selection and put it into the clipboard.
Ctrl+V	Paste data in clipboard as new image.
Ctrl+L	Paste the clipboard contents into the current document as a new layer.
Ctrl+E	Paste data in the clipboard into the current image as a new selection.
Ctrl+G	Paste vector data in clipboard into the current image as a new vector selection.

Ctrl+Shift+E	Paste data from clipboard into the current image using the background colour as transparent.
Ctrl+Shift+L	Paste data from clipboard into the selected area.
Ctrl+Alt+Z	Redo the last command..
Ctrl+Y	Repeat the last action.
Ctrl+Z	Undo the last command.

View Menu

Shift+A	Edit the current document using all available screen space.
Ctrl+Shift+A	View the current document full screen (Press <Esc> to exit preview mode).
Ctrl+Alt+G	Show Grid.
Ctrl+Alt+M	Show or hide the Tool Magnifier window.
F11	Show or hide the Brush Variance palette.
F7	Show or hide the Histogram palette.
F8	Show or hide the Layers palette.
F10	Show or hide the Learning Center palette.
F6	Show or hide the Materials palette.
F9	Show or hide the Overview palette.
F3	Show or hide the Script Output palette.
F4	Show or hide the Tool Options palette.
Ctrl+Alt+R	Shows/hides rulers.
Ctrl+Shift+G	Snaps position to the grid.
Shift+Alt+G	Snaps position to the guides.
Num plus	Zoom in by 1 Step (Increases the apparent size).
Num sub	Zoom out by 1 Step (Decreases the apparent size).
Ctrl+Alt+N	View the image normally, with no zoom factor.

Image Menu

Shift+R	Crop Tool, used to eliminate or crop areas around an image.
Ctrl+Shift+1	Decrease the number of colours to 2.
Ctrl+Shift+2	Decrease the number of colours to 16.
Ctrl+Shift+3	Decrease the number of colours to 256.
Ctrl+Shift+4	Decrease the number of colours to 32K.
Ctrl+Shift+5	Decrease the number of colours to 64K.
Ctrl+Shift+6	Decrease the number of colours to a value you select.
Ctrl+I	Flip image.
Shift+I	View details about the current image.
Ctrl+Shift+8	Increase the number of colours to 16.
Ctrl+Shift+0	Increase the number of colours to 16 million (24 bit).
Ctrl+Shift+9	Increase the number of colours to 256.
Ctrl+M	Apply mirror to image.
Shift+P	Edit the palette for the current picture.
Shift+O	Load a palette from disc, and apply to the current image.
Shift+S	Change the size of the image.
Ctrl+R	Apply rotation to image.

Adjust Menu

Shift+B	Adjust brightness and/or contrast.
Shift+G	Apply gamma correction to the image.
Shift+M	Adjust the brightness of the highlights and shadows.
Ctrl+Shift+H	Adjust the image while viewing the histogram.
Shift+E	Equalise the relative brightness of the current image.
Shift+T	Stretch the contrast of the current image so that all possible values are used.

Shift+U	Adjust the red, green, and/or blue.
Shift+L	Colorise the image.

Layers Menu

Shift+K	Invert the current mask or adjustment layer.
Shift+Y	Make a new mask that obscures the entire layer.

Selections Menu

Ctrl+Shift+F	Place the current floating selection into the image.
Ctrl+F	Convert the current regular selection into a floating selection.
Ctrl+Shift+S	Create a new selection from the current mask channel.
Ctrl+Shift+B	Create a Raster Selection from a Vector Selection.
Ctrl+Shift+M	Keep the selection marquee from appearing on the image.
Ctrl+Shift+I	Invert the current selection area.
Ctrl+H	Feather the existing selection.
Ctrl+Shift+P	Promote a floating selection to a new layer.
Ctrl+A	Select entire image.
Ctrl+D	Remove the current selection.

Help Menu

Shift+F1	Display Help for clicked-on buttons, menus and windows.
F10	Show or hide the Learning Center palette.

Window Menu

Shift+D	Duplicate the current image.
Ctrl+W	Fit the window to the image.
Shift+W	Open another window for the active document.

Other Commands

Ctrl+K	Edit the closest mask layer.
F2	Hide the palettes.
Ctrl+Num plus	Magnify Window Zoom In.
Ctrl+Num minus	Magnify Window Zoom Out.
Ctrl+Shift+F6	Reset materials to solid black and white.
Ctrl+Shift+T	Show all toolbars.
Ctrl+Alt+F6	Swap foreground and background materials in the Materials palette.
Ctrl+Alt+V	View the image through the current mask.

Brushes and Tools

C	**Clone Brush**: Use to create brush strokes that duplicate part of an image.
R	**Crop Tool**: Use to eliminate or crop areas of an image.
D	**Deform Tool**: Use to rotate, resize, skew, and distort layers or images.
J	**Dodge Brush**: Use to bring out details in areas that are in shadow.
E	**Dropper Tool**: Use to select active foreground and background colours.
X	**Eraser Tool**: Use to replace colours in image with background colour or transparency.

F	**Flood Fill Tool**: Use to fill an area with a colour, pattern, or gradient.
L	**Lighten/Darken Brush**: Use to increase or decrease lightness (affects HSL value).
M	**Move Tool**: Use to move a layer or selection marquee.
O	**Object Selection Tool**: Use to select, move, resize, reshape, and rotate vector objects.
B	**Paint Brush**: Use to paint strokes on a raster layer.
A	**Pan Tool**: Use to pan large images.
V	**Pen Tool**: Draws lines, polylines, point to point, and freehand
I	**Picture Tube Tool**: Use to paint with pictures.
P	**Preset Shape Tool**: Use to draw shapes as raster or vector objects on raster or vector layers.
S	**Selection Tool**: Use to create selections of precise shapes.
T	**Text Tool**: Use to create raster or vector text on raster or vector layers.
Z	**Zoom Tool**: Use to zoom in and out of images.

If you would like more detail on actually using Paint Shop Pro 8, then may we suggest you keep a lookout for our book BP545, *Paint Shop Pro 8 explained*, also published by BERNARD BABANI (publishing) Ltd.

16

Adobe Reader 6

Adobe® Reader is a free software package that lets you view and print Portable Document Format **.pdf** files on almost any combination of hardware and operating system.

Version 6.0 of the Reader comes with features that enable you to:

- Fill in and submit **.pdf** forms.
- Play back embedded multimedia content, such as QuickTime video and MP3 music files.
- Read and work with eBooks.
- Use the search and accessibility options built into your **.pdf** files.

You can download the latest version of the Reader from the following Web page:

http://www.adobe.co.uk/products/acrobat/readstep2.html

What is PDF

Portable Document Format (**pdf**) was developed by Adobe over ten years ago and has become the standard for the secure and reliable distribution and exchange of electronic documents and forms around the world. It is a universal file format that preserves the fonts, images, graphics, and layout of a source document, regardless of the platform and application used to create it.

.pdf files are compact and can be shared, viewed, and printed by anyone with free Adobe Reader software. To date, more than 500 million copies of this software have been distributed.

.pdf is an open file format specification, which is available to anyone who wants to develop tools to create, view, or manipulate **.pdf** documents.

At one stage in its life this book was in the form of a **.pdf** file. We authors created and formatted it, and then converted it to **pdf** format so that the printers could load it straight into their printing software.

The following is a list of Adobe Reader 6 keyboard shortcuts, many require you to press two keys. For example, **Ctrl+A** means hold down the **Ctrl** key and press the letter **A**.

Menu Command Shortcuts

Many of Adobe Reader 6's keyboard shortcuts are listed on the program's main sub-menus.

File Menu

Ctrl+O	Open a **pdf** file.
Ctrl+W	Close the current file.
Shift+Ctrl+S	Save a copy of the current file.
Ctrl+D	Open the Document Properties box.
Ctrl+P	Open the Print dialogue box.
Shift+Ctrl+P	Set up the printer.
Alt+Ctrl+P	Print via the Internet, or set up to do it.
Ctrl+Q	Exit the program.

Edit Menu

Ctrl+X	Cut selection to the clipboard.
Ctrl+C	Copy selection to the clipboard.
Ctrl+V	Paste clipboard contents.
Ctrl+Z	Undo the last command.
Shift+Ctrl+Z	Redo the last command.
Ctrl+A	Select all of the current page.
Shift+Ctrl+A	De-select all.
Ctrl+F	Start a search operation.
Ctrl+]	Search next document.
Ctrl+[	Search previous document.
Ctrl+G	Next search result.
Shift+Ctrl+G	Previous search result.
Ctrl+K	Open the Preferences dialogue box.

View Menu

F6	Open or close the Navigation pane.
F4	Open or close the How To pane.
Ctrl+E	Open or close the Properties toolbar.
F8	Hide the toolbars.
Alt+Ctrl+D	Dock all toolbars.
F9	Display or hide the main menu bar.
Ctrl+M	Open the Zoom To dialogue box.
Ctrl+1	Zoom to actual size.
Ctrl+0	Zoom to fit whole page in window.
Ctrl+2	Zoom to fit page width in window.
Ctrl+3	Zoom to fit margin width within window.
Ctrl+4	Reflow text.
Shift+Ctrl+H	Start or stop automatic scrolling of text.
Shift+Ctrl+V	Read current page out loud.
Shift+Ctrl+B	Read the rest of the document out loud.
Shift+Ctrl+C	Pause reading document out loud.
Shift+Ctrl+E	Stop reading out loud.
Home	Go to document first page.
⇐	Previous page.
⇨	Next page.
End	Last page.
Shift+Ctrl+N	Go to a specific page number.
Alt+ ⇐	Go back to previous view.
Alt+ ⇨	Go to next view.
Alt+Shift+ ⇐	Go to previous document.
Alt+Shift+ ⇨	Go to next document.
Shift+Ctrl+Plus	Rotate view clockwise.
Shift+Ctrl+Minus	Rotate view anti-clockwise.

Window Menu

Shift+Ctrl+J	Show open windows in cascade view.
Shift+Ctrl+K	Tile open windows horizontally.
Shift+Ctrl+L	Tile open windows vertically.
Shift+Ctrl+W	Close all open documents or windows.
Ctrl+L	Show document in Full Screen view.

Main Keyboard Shortcuts

Before you can use the following shortcuts, you must use the **Ctrl+K** shortcut to open the Preferences dialogue box, click the General link, select the **Use single-key accelerators to access tools** option and then press **OK**.

Shortcuts for Selecting Tools

H	**Hand** tool.
Spacebar	Temporarily select **Hand** tool.
V	Current selection tool.
Shift+V	Cycle through selection tools: **Select Text**, **Select Image** and **Select Table**.
G	**Snapshot** tool.
Shift+Z	Cycle through zoom tools: **Zoom In**, **Zoom Out** and **Dynamic Zoom**.
Z	Current zoom tool.
Ctrl+Space	Temporarily select **Zoom In** tool.
Shift	Temporarily select **Dynamic Zoom** tool (when **Zoom In** or **Zoom Out** is being used).

Moving Through a Document

Page Up	Previous screen.
Page Down	Next screen.
Home	First page.
Up Arrow	Scroll up.
Down Arrow	Scroll down.
Space	Scroll (when Hand tool is selected).
Ctrl+plus	Zoom in.
Ctrl+minus	Zoom out.
Ctrl+Space	Zoom in temporarily.

Working with Comments

S	**Note** tool.
K	**Stamp** tool.
U	Current highlighting tool.
Shift+U	Cycle through highlighting tools: **Highlighter**, **Cross-Out Text** and **Underline Text**.
J	**Attach File** tool.
Tab	Move focus to comment.
Space	Open pop-up window for comment that has focus.

General Navigation

F9	Show/hide menu bar.
F10	Move focus to menus.
Alt, then Ctrl+Tab	Move focus to toolbar area.
Ctrl+Tab	Move focus to next toolbar.
Shift+F8	Move focus to toolbar in browser or the Help window.
Ctrl+I	Open Properties toolbar, or Properties dialogue box.

Ctrl+F6	Cycle through open documents (when focus is on document pane).
Alt+F6	Move focus to next floating panel, or open dialogue box.
Tab or ⇨	Move focus to next field or item in the document pane.
Shift+Tab or ⇦	Move focus to previous field or item in the document pane.
Space or Enter	Activate selected tool, item (such as a movie or bookmark), or command.
Shift+F10	Open/close context menu.
Esc	Close an open menu, context menu, or dialogue box.
Shift+Ctrl+W	Close all windows.
Ctrl+Tab	Move focus to next tab in a tabbed dialogue box.
F3	Move to next search result and highlight it in the document.
Shift+arrow keys	Select text (when **Select Text** tool is active).
Shift+Ctrl+⇨/⇦	Select previous/next word (when **Select Text** tool is active).
Ctrl+⇨/⇦	Move cursor to next/previous word (when **Select Text** tool is active).

Working with Navigation Tabs

F6	Open/close navigation pane.
Shift+F6	Move focus between navigation pane and document pane.
Tab	Move focus to next element of the active navigation tab: Trash Can, Options menu, Close box, tab contents, and tab.
⇧ or ⇩	Move to next navigation tab and make it active (when focus is on the tab).

Ctrl+Tab	Move to next navigation tab and make it active (focus is in the navigation pane).
⇒ or Shift+plus	Expand the current bookmark (focus is on the Bookmarks tab).
⇐ or minus	Collapse the current bookmark (focus is on the Bookmarks tab).
F2	Rename selected bookmark.
Shift+*	Expand all bookmarks.
/	Collapse selected bookmark.
Tab or ⇓	Move focus to next item in navigation tab.
Shift+Tab or ⇑	Move focus to previous item in a navigation tab.

The Help Window

F1	Open/close Help window.
Shift+F8	Move focus to toolbar in Help window.
⇒ or ⇐	Move focus among tabs: Contents, Search, Index.
Tab	Toggle focus between active tab and tab contents.
⇑ or ⇓	Move to next element in active tab.
Shift+F4	Reflow the Help document.

The How To Pane

F4	Open the How To pane.
F4 or Esc	Close the How To pane.
Shift+F4	Move focus between How To pane and document pane.
Home	Go to How To home page.
Shift+Ctrl+Tab	Move focus among the elements of the How To pane.
⇒	Go to next page in How To pane.
⇐	Go to previous page in How To pane.

Shortcuts in Internet Explorer

You can use the keyboard to control the Reader when it is working within Microsoft Internet Explorer window. At first, the focus is on the Web browser, so any keyboard shortcuts you use act according to their Internet Explorer functions.

Pressing the **Tab** key shifts the focus from the browser to the Reader and its document. Navigation and command keystrokes will then function normally.

Pressing **Ctrl+Tab** at any time shifts the focus from the document back to Internet Explorer.

Scrolling Automatically

The automatic scrolling feature, activated with the **View**, **Automatically Scroll** menu command or **Shift+Ctrl+H**, makes it easier to scan through a long document. In this mode you can use the following keyboard shortcuts:

0 to 9, or ⇧/⇩	Change the scrolling speed. With the number keys - 9 is the fastest and 0 is the slowest. We find it easier to use the Up and Down arrow keys.
—	Reverse the direction of the scrolling.
⇐ or ⇒	Jump to the next or previous page.
Esc	Stop automatic scrolling.

17

Adobe Acrobat 6

The previous chapter introduced **.pdf** files and listed the keyboard shortcuts in the freely available Adobe Reader application. In this chapter we cover Adobe Acrobat the program mostly used to create .**pdf** files in the first place.

About Adobe Acrobat

Acrobat lets you easily create a fully searchable **.pdf** file from any electronic document, from paper scans, and from Web pages. You can even convert Microsoft Office files to .**pdf** with one button click. With it you can add page numbers, headers, footers, and watermarks to a **.pdf** file and then e-mail it to colleagues or clients who can use the Adobe Reader software to view and print the document with its layout, fonts and images intact. We use this format to send the copy of our books to the printers, and it does not matter what software they use, as the style and format is maintained.

Acrobat 6.0 has quite powerful document review and commenting tools built into it. You can create a list of reviewers and then track feedback to help you meet critical deadlines. A how-to pane helps reviewers engage in the review process and quickly get up to speed. Reviewers can comment straight onto the document with intuitive electronic tools, or can respond to comments directly on the page.

Using password protection, you can restrict access to sensitive or confidential files. 128-bit encryption lets you specify what authorised users can do with your **.pdf** files, such as copy and extract information, print the document, comment on, or digitally sign it.

The following is a list of Adobe Acrobat 6 keyboard shortcuts, many require you to press two keys. For example, **Ctrl+A** means hold down the **Ctrl** key and press the letter **A**.

Menu Command Shortcuts

Many of Acrobat 6's keyboard shortcuts are listed on the program's main sub-menus.

File Menu

Ctrl+N	Create a **.pdf** from an existing file.
Shift+Ctrl+O	Create a **.pdf** from a Web page.
Ctrl+O	Open an existing **.pdf** file.
Ctrl+W	Close the current file.
Ctrl+S	Save the current file with the same name.
Shift+Ctrl+S	Save the current file with a new name.
Ctrl+D	Open the Document Properties box.
Ctrl+P	Open the Print dialogue box.
Shift+Ctrl+P	Set up the printer.
Ctrl+T	Print the document with comments.
Alt+Ctrl+P	Print via the Internet, or set up to do it.
Ctrl+Q	Exit the program.

Edit Menu

Ctrl+X	Cut selection to the clipboard.
Ctrl+C	Copy selection to the clipboard.
Ctrl+V	Paste clipboard contents.
Ctrl+Z	Undo the last command.
Shift+Ctrl+Z	Redo the last command.
Ctrl+A	Select all of the current page.
Shift+Ctrl+A	De-select all.

F7	Check spelling in comments and form fields.
Ctrl+B	Add a bookmark.
Ctrl+F	Start a search operation.
Ctrl+]	Search next document.
Ctrl+[	Search previous document.
Ctrl+G	Next search result.
Shift+Ctrl+G	Previous search result.
Ctrl+K	Open the Preferences dialogue box.

View Menu

F6	Open or close the Navigation pane.
F4	Open or close the How To pane.
Ctrl+E	Open or close the Properties toolbar.
F8	Hide the toolbars.
Alt+Ctrl+D	Dock all toolbars.
F9	Display or hide the main menu bar.
Ctrl+M	Open the Zoom To dialogue box.
Ctrl+1	Zoom to actual size.
Ctrl+0	Zoom to fit whole page in window.
Ctrl+2	Zoom to fit page width in window.
Ctrl+3	Zoom to fit margin width within window.
Ctrl+4	Reflow text.
Shift+Ctrl+H	Start or stop automatic scrolling of text.
Shift+Ctrl+V	Read current page out loud.
Shift+Ctrl+B	Read the rest of the document out loud.
Shift+Ctrl+C	Pause reading document out loud.
Shift+Ctrl+E	Stop reading out loud.
Home	Go to document first page.
⇐	Previous page.
⇒	Next page.
End	Last page.
Shift+Ctrl+N	Go to a specific page number.

Alt+ ⇐	Go back to previous view.
Alt+ ⇒	Go to next view.
Alt+Shift+ ⇐	Go to previous document.
Alt+Shift+ ⇒	Go to next document.
Shift+Ctrl+Plus	Rotate view clockwise.
Shift+Ctrl+Minus	Rotate view anti-clockwise.

Document Menu

Shift+Ctrl+I	Insert pages into current document.
Shift+Ctrl+D	Delete pages from current document.
Shift+Ctrl+T	Open the Crop Pages dialogue box.
Shift+Ctrl+R	Open the Rotate Pages dialogue box.

Advanced Menu

Shift+Ctrl+Y	Use local fonts.
Alt+Shift+Ctrl+Y	Gives an Overprint Preview to simulate how colour separated work will print.

Window Menu

Shift+Ctrl+J	Show open windows in cascade view.
Shift+Ctrl+K	Tile open windows horizontally.
Shift+Ctrl+L	Tile open windows vertically.
Shift+Ctrl+W	Close all open documents or windows.
Ctrl+L	Show document in Full Screen view.

Main Keyboard Shortcuts

Before you can use the following shortcuts, you must use the **Ctrl+K** shortcut to open the Preferences dialogue box, click the General link, select the **Use single-key accelerators to access tools** option and then press **OK**.

Shortcuts for Selecting Tools

H	**Hand** tool.
Spacebar	Temporarily select **Hand** tool.
V	Current selection tool.
Shift+V	Cycle through selection tools: **Select Text**, **Select Image** and **Select Table**.
G	**Snapshot** tool.
Shift+Z	Cycle through zoom tools: **Zoom In**, **Zoom Out** and **Dynamic Zoom**.
Z	Current zoom tool.
Ctrl+Space	Temporarily select **Zoom In** tool.
Shift	Temporarily select **Dynamic Zoom** tool (when **Zoom In** or **Zoom Out** is being used).
R	**Select Object** tool.
A	**Article** tool.
C	**Crop** tool.
L	**Link** tool.
T	**Touch Up Text** tool.

Moving Through a Document

Page Up	Previous screen.
Page Down	Next screen.
Home	First page.

Up Arrow	Scroll up.
Down Arrow	Scroll down.
Space	Scroll (when Hand tool is selected).
Ctrl+plus	Zoom in.
Ctrl+minus	Zoom out.
Ctrl+Space	Zoom in temporarily.

Working with Comments

S	**Note** tool.
E	**Text Edits** tool.
K	**Stamp** tool.
U	Current highlighting tool.
Shift+U	Cycle through highlighting tools: **Highlighter**, **Cross-Out Text** and **Underline Text**.
D	Current drawing tool.
Shift+D	Cycle through drawing tools: **Rectangle**, **Oval**, **Line**, **Polygon**, **Polygon Line**.
X	**Text Box** tool.
N	**Pencil** tool.
Shift+N	**Pencil Eraser** tool.
J	Current attach tool.
Shift+J	Cycle through attach tools: **Attach File**, **Attach Sound**, **Paste Clipboard Image**.
Tab	Move focus to comment.
Space	Open pop-up window for comment.
Q	Send comments.
O	Send and receive comments in browser-based review.
W	Mark document status as complete in browser-based review.
Y	Save document and work off-line (browser-based review).
I	Go back on-line.

General Navigation

F9	Show/hide menu bar.
F10	Move focus to menus.
Alt, then Ctrl+Tab	Move focus to toolbar area.
Ctrl+Tab	Move focus to next toolbar.
Shift+F8	Move focus to toolbar in browser or the Help window.
Ctrl+I	Open Properties toolbar, or Properties dialogue box.
Ctrl+F6	Cycle through open documents (when focus is on document pane).
Alt+F6	Move focus to next floating panel, or open dialogue box.
Tab or ⇨	Move focus to next field or item in the document pane.
Shift+Tab or ⇦	Move focus to previous field or item in the document pane.
Space or Enter	Activate selected tool, item (such as a movie or bookmark), or command.
Shift+F10	Open/close context menu.
Esc	Close an open menu, context menu, or dialogue box.
Shift+Ctrl+W	Close all windows.
Ctrl+Tab	Move focus to next tab in a tabbed dialogue box.
F3	Move to next search result and highlight it in the document.
Shift+arrow keys	Select text (when **Select Text** tool is active).
Shift+Ctrl+ ⇨/⇦	Select previous/next word (when **Select Text** tool is active).
Ctrl+ ⇨/⇦	Move cursor to next/previous word (when **Select Text** tool is active).

Working with Navigation Tabs

F6	Open/close navigation pane.
Shift+F6	Move focus between navigation pane and document pane.
Tab	Move focus to next element of the active navigation tab: Trash Can, Options menu, Close box, tab contents, and tab.
⇧ or ⇩	Move to next navigation tab and make it active (when focus is on the tab).
Ctrl+Tab	Move to next navigation tab and make it active (focus anywhere in the navigation pane).
⇒ or Shift+plus	Expand the current bookmark (when focus is on the Bookmarks tab).
⇐ or minus	Collapse the current bookmark (when focus is on the Bookmarks tab).
F2	Rename selected bookmark.
Shift+*	Expand all bookmarks.
/	Collapse selected bookmark.
Tab or ⇩	Move focus to next item in a navigation tab.
Shift+Tab or ⇧	Move focus to previous item in a navigation tab.

The Help Window

F1	Open/close Help window.
Shift+F8	Move focus to toolbar in Help window.
⇒ or ⇐	Move focus among tabs: Contents, Search, Index.
Tab	Toggle focus between active tab and tab contents.
⇧ or ⇩	Move to next element in active tab.
Shift+F4	Reflow the Help document.

The How To Pane

F4	Open the How To pane.
F4 or Esc	Close the How To pane.
Shift+F4	Move focus between How To pane and document pane.
Home	Go to How To home page.
Shift+Ctrl+Tab	Move focus among the elements of the How To pane.
⇨	Go to next page in How To pane.
⇦	Go to previous page in How To pane.

Shortcuts in Internet Explorer

You can use the keyboard to control Acrobat within Microsoft Internet Explorer. At first, the focus is on the Web browser, so any keyboard shortcuts you use act according to their Internet Explorer functions. Pressing the **Tab** key shifts the focus from the browser to the Acrobat and its document. Navigation and command keystrokes will then function normally. Pressing **Ctrl+Tab** at any time shifts the focus from the document back to Internet Explorer.

Scrolling Automatically

The automatic scrolling feature, activated with the **View**, **Automatically Scroll** menu command or **Shift+Ctrl+H**, makes it easier to scan through a long document. In this mode you can use the following keyboard shortcuts:

0 to 9, or ⇧/⇩	Change the scrolling speed. With the number keys 9 is the fastest and 0 is the slowest.
—	Reverse the direction of the scrolling.
⇦ or ⇨	Jump to the next or previous page.
Esc	Stop automatic scrolling.

18

Glossary of Terms

Active	Describes the folder, window or icon that you are currently using or that is currently selected.
Add-in	A mini-program which runs in conjunction with another and enhances its functionality.
Address	A unique number or name that identifies a specific computer or user on a network.
Administrator	For Windows XP Professional, a person responsible for setting up and managing local computers, their user and group accounts, and assigning passwords and permissions.
Anonymous FTP	Anonymous FTP allows you to connect to a remote computer and transfer public files back to your local computer without the need to have a user ID and password.
Applet	A program that can be downloaded over a network and launched on the user's computer.
Application	Software (program) designed to carry out a certain activity, such as word processing, or data management.
ASCII	A binary code representation of a character set. The name stands for 'American Standard Code for Information Interchange'.

Association	An identification of a filename extension to a program. This lets Windows open the program when its files are selected.
Audio input device	A device that records music and voice input into your computer, such as a microphone or a CD-ROM player.
Authentication	The process for verifying that an entity or object is who or what it claims to be.
Authoring	The process of creating web documents or software.
Background	The screen background image used on a graphical user interface such as Windows.
Backup	To make a back-up copy of a file or a disc for safekeeping.
Bandwidth	The range of transmission frequencies a network can use. The greater the bandwidth the more information that can be transferred over a network.
Banner	An advertising graphic shown on a Web page.
BASIC	Beginner's All-purpose Symbolic Instruction Code - a high-level programming language.
Basic volume	A primary partition or logical drive that resides on a basic disc.
Baud rate	The speed at which a modem communicates.

Beta test	A test of software that is still under development, by people actually using the software.
Binary	A base-2 number system in which values are expressed as combinations of two digits, 0 and 1.
BIOS	On x86-based computers, the set of software routines that test hardware at startup, start the operating system, and support the transfer of data among hardware devices.
Bit	The smallest unit of information handled by a computer.
Bitmap	A technique for managing the image displayed on a computer screen.
Bookmark	A marker inserted at a specific point in a document to which the user may wish to return for later reference.
Boot up	To start your computer by switching it on, which initiates a self test of its Random Access Memory (RAM), then loads the necessary system files.
Broadband	A communications systems in which the medium of transmission (such as a wire or fibre-optic cable) carries multiple messages at a time.
Broadcast	An address that is destined for all hosts on a particular network segment.
Browse	A button in some Windows dialogue boxes that lets you view a list of files and folders before you make a selection.

Browser	A program, like Internet Explorer, that lets you view Web pages.
Bug	An error in coding or logic that causes a program to malfunction.
Bus	A communication line used for data transfer among the components of a computer system.
Button	A graphic element in a dialogue box or toolbar that performs a specified function.
Byte	A unit of data that holds a single character, such as a letter, a digit.
Cache	An area of memory, or disc space, reserved for data, which speeds up downloading.
Card	A removable printed-circuit board that is plugged into a computer expansion slot.
CD-R	Recordable compact disc.
CD-ROM	Read Only Memory compact disc. Data can be read but not written.
CD-RW	Rewritable compact disc. Data can be copied to the CD on more than one occasion and can be erased.
Chart	A graphical view of data that is used to visually display trends, patterns, and comparisons.
Click	To press and release a mouse button once without moving the mouse.
Client	A computer that has access to services over a computer network. The computer providing the services is a server.

Client application | A Windows application that can accept linked, or embedded, objects.

Clipboard | A temporary storage area of memory, where text and graphics are stored with the Windows cut and copy actions.

Cluster | In data storage, the smallest amount of disc space that can be allocated to hold a file.

Code page | A means of providing support for character sets and keyboard layouts for different countries or regions.

Command | An instruction given to a computer to carry out a particular action.

Compressed file | One that is compacted to save server space and reduce transfer times. Typical file extensions for compressed files include .zip (DOS/Windows) and .tar (UNIX).

Configuration | A general purpose term referring to the way you have your computer set up.

Controls | Objects on a form, report, or data access page that display data, perform actions, or are used for decoration.

Cookies | Files stored on your hard drive by your Web browser that hold information for it to use.

CPU | The Central Processing Unit; the main chip that executes all instructions entered into a computer.

Cyberspace | Originated by William Gibson in his novel 'Neuromancer', now used to

	describe the Internet and the other computer networks.
Data access page	A Web page, created by Access, that has a connection to a database; you can view, add, edit, and manipulate the data in this page.
Data packet	A unit of information transmitted as a whole from one device to another on a network.
Database	A collection of data related to a particular topic or purpose.
DBMS	Database management system - A software interface between the database and the user.
Default	The command, device or option automatically chosen.
Defragmentation	The process of rewriting parts of a file to contiguous sectors on a hard disc to increase the speed of access and retrieval.
Desktop	The Windows screen working background, on which you place icons, folders, etc.
Device driver	A special file that must be loaded into memory for Windows to be able to address a specific procedure or hardware device.
Device name	A logical name used by DOS to identify a device, such as LPT1 or COM1 for the parallel or serial printer.
Dial-up connection	The connection to a network via a device that uses the telephone network. This includes modems with a standard phone line, ISDN cards

	with high-speed ISDN lines, or X.25 networks.
Dialogue box	A window displayed on the screen to allow the user to enter information.
Direct Connection	A permanent connection between your computer system and the Internet.
Directory	An area on disc where information relating to a group of files is kept. Also known as a folder.
Disconnect	To detach a drive, port or computer from a shared device, or to break an Internet connection.
Display adapter	An expansion board that plugs into a PC to give it display capabilities.
DLL	Dynamic Link Library; An OS feature that allows files with the .dll extensions to be loaded only when needed by the program.
Document	A file produced by an application program. When used in reference to the Web, a document is any file containing text, media or hyperlinks that can be transferred from an HTTP server to a browser.
Domain	A group of devices, servers and computers on a network.
Domain Name	The name of an Internet site, for example www.microsoft.com, which allows you to reference Internet sites without knowing their true numerical address.
DOS	Disc Operating System. A collection of small specialised programs that

	allow interaction between user and computer.
Double-click	To quickly press and release a mouse button twice.
Download	To transfer to your computer a file, or data, from another computer.
DPI	Dots Per Inch - a resolution standard for laser printers.
Drag	To move an object on the screen by pressing and holding down the left mouse button while moving the mouse.
Drive name	The letter followed by a colon which identifies a floppy or hard disc drive.
DSL	Digital Subscriber Line - a broad-band connection to the Internet through existing copper telephone wires.
DVD	Digital Video Disc; a type of optical disc technology. It looks like a CD but can store greater amounts of data.
E-mail	Electronic Mail - A system that allows computer users to send and receive messages electronically.
Embedded object	Information in a document that is 'copied' from its source application. Selecting the object opens the creating application from within the document.
Encrypted password	A password that is scrambled.
Engine	Software used by search services.
Ethernet	A very common method of networking computers in a LAN.

Expansion slot	A socket in a computer, designed to hold expansion boards and connect them to the system bus.
FAQ	Frequently Asked Questions - A common feature on the Internet, FAQs are files of answers to commonly asked questions.
FAT	The File Allocation Table. An area on disc where information is kept on which part of the disc a file is located.
File extension	The suffix following the period in a filename. Windows uses this to identify the source application program. For example .mdb indicates an Access file.
Filename	The name given to a file. In Windows 95 and above this can be up to 256 characters long.
Filter	A set of criteria that is applied to data to show a subset of the data.
Firewall	Security measures designed to protect a networked system from unauthorised access.
Floppy disc	A removable disc on which information can be stored magnetically.
Folder	An area used to store a group of files, usually with a common link.
Font	A graphic design representing a set of characters, numbers and symbols.
Format	The structure of a file that defines the way it is stored and laid out on the screen or in print.

Fragmentation	The scattering of parts of the same file over different areas of the disc.
Free space	Available disc space that can be used to create logical drives within an extended partition.
Freeware	Software that is available for downloading and unlimited use without charge.
FTP	File Transfer Protocol. The procedure for connecting to a remote computer and transferring files.
Function key	One of the series of 10 or 12 keys marked with the letter F and a numeral, used for specific operations.
Gateway	A computer system that allows otherwise incompatible networks to communicate with each other.
GIF	Graphics Interchange Format, a common standard for images on the Web.
Gigabyte	(GB); 1,024 megabytes. Usually thought of as one billion bytes.
Graphic	A picture or illustration, also called an image. Formats include GIF, JPEG, BMP, PCX, and TIFF.
Graphics card	A device that controls the display on the monitor and other allied functions.
Group	A collection of users, computers, contacts, and other groups.
GUI	A Graphic User Interface, such as Windows, the software front-end meant to provide an attractive and easy to use interface.

Handshaking	A series of signals acknowledging that communication can take place between computers or other devices.
Hard copy	Output on paper.
Hard disc	A device built into the computer for holding programs and data.
Hardware	The equipment that makes up a computer system, excluding the programs or software.
Help	A Windows system that gives you instructions and additional information on using a program.
Hibernation	A state in which your computer shuts down after saving everything in memory onto your hard disc.
Home page	The document displayed when you first open your Web browser, or the first document you come to at a Web site.
Host	Computer connected directly to the Internet that provides services to other local and/or remote computers.
HTML	HyperText Markup Language, the format used in documents on the Web.
HTML editor	Authoring tool which assists with the creation of HTML pages.
HTTP	HyperText Transport Protocol, the system used to link and transfer hypertext documents on the Web.
Hub	A common connection point for devices in a network.

Hyperlink	A segment of text, or an image, that refers to another document on the Web, an intranet or your PC.
Hypermedia	Hypertext extended to include linked multimedia.
Hypertext	A system that allows documents to be cross-linked so that the reader can explore related links, or documents, by clicking on a highlighted symbol.
Icon	A small graphic image that represents a function or object. Clicking on an icon produces an action.
Image	See graphic.
Insertion point	A flashing bar that shows where typed text will be entered into a document.
Interface	A device that allows you to connect a computer to its peripherals.
Internet	The global system of computer networks.
Intranet	A private network inside an organisation using the same kind of software as the Internet.
IP	Internet Protocol - The rules that provide basic Internet functions.
IP Address	Internet Protocol Address - every computer on the Internet has a unique identifying number.
ISA	Industry Standard Architecture; a standard for internal PC connections.
ISDN	Integrated Services Digital Network; a telecom standard using digital

transmission technology to support voice, video and data communications applications over regular telephone lines.

ISP
Internet Service Provider - A company that offers access to the Internet.

Java
An object-oriented programming language created by Sun Microsystems for developing applications and applets that are capable of running on any computer, regardless of the operating system.

JPEG / JPG
Joint Photographic Experts Group, a popular cross-platform format for image files. JPEG is best suited for true colour original images.

Kernel
The core of layered architecture that manages the most basic operations of the operating system and the computer's processor.

Kilobyte
(KB); 1024 bytes of information or storage space.

LAN
Local Area Network - High-speed, privately-owned network covering a limited geographical area, such as an office or a building.

Laptop
A portable computer small enough to sit on your lap.

LCD
Liquid Crystal Display.

Linked object
An object that is inserted into a document but still exists in the source file. Changing the original object automatically updates it within the linked document.

Links	The hypertext connections between Web pages.
Linux	A version of the UNIX operating system for PCs which incorporates a Graphical User Interface (GUI) similar to that of Microsoft Windows.
Local	A resource that is located on your computer, not linked to it over a network.
Location	An Internet address.
Log on	To gain access to a network.
MCI	Media Control Interface - a standard for files and multimedia devices.
Megabyte	(MB); 1024 kilobytes of information or storage space.
Megahertz	(MHz); Speed of processor in millions of cycles per second.
Memory	Part of computer consisting of storage elements organised into addressable locations that can hold data and instructions.
Menu	A list of available options in an application.
Menu bar	The horizontal bar that lists the names of menus.
MIDI	Musical Instrument Digital Interface - enables devices to transmit and receive sound and music messages.
MIME	Multipurpose Internet Mail Extensions, a messaging standard that allows Internet users to exchange e-mail messages

	enhanced with graphics, video and voice.
MIPS	Million Instructions Per Second; measures speed of a system.
Modem	Short for Modulator-demodulator. An electronic device that lets computers communicate electronically.
Monitor	The display device connected to your PC, also called a screen.
Mouse	A device used to manipulate a pointer around your display and activate processes by pressing buttons.
MPEG	Motion Picture Experts Group - a video file format offering excellent quality in a relatively small file.
MS-DOS	Microsoft's implementation of the Disc Operating System for PCs.
Multimedia	The use of photographs, music and sound and movie images in a presentation.
Multitasking	Performing more than one operation at the same time.
My Documents	A folder that provides a convenient place to store documents, graphics, or other files you want to access quickly.
Network	Two or more computers connected together to share resources.
Network adapter	A device that connects your computer to a network.
Network server	Central computer which stores files for several linked computers.

Node	Any single computer connected to a network.
NTFS file system	An advanced file system that provides performance, security, reliability, and advanced features that are not found in any version of FAT.
ODBC	Open DataBase Connectivity - A standard protocol for accessing information in a SQL database server.
OLE	Object Linking and Embedding - A technology for transferring and sharing information among software applications.
Online	Having access to the Internet.
On-line Service	Services such as America On-line and CompuServe that provide content to subscribers and usually connections to the Internet.
Operating system	Software that runs a computer.
Page	An HTML document, or Web site.
Parallel port	The input/output connector for a parallel interface device. Printers are generally plugged into a parallel port.
Partition	A portion of a physical disc that functions as though it were a physically separate disc.
Password	A unique character string used to gain access to a network, program, or mailbox.
PATH	The location of a file in the directory tree.

PCI	Peripheral Component Interconnect - a type of slot in your computer which accepts similar type peripheral cards.
Peripheral	Any device attached to a PC.
Perl	A popular language for programming CGI applications.
PIF file	Program information file - gives information to Windows about an MS-DOS application.
Pixel	A picture element on screen; the smallest element that can be independently assigned colour and intensity.
Plug-and-play	Hardware which can be plugged into a PC and be used immediately without configuration.
POP	Post Office Protocol - a method of storing and returning e-mail.
Port	The place where information goes into or out of a computer, e.g. a modem might be connected to the serial port.
Posix	The specification for a look-alike UNIX operating system drawn up by the American National Standards Institute (ANSI). Linux is an independent Posix implementation.
PostScript	A page-description language (PDL), developed by Adobe Systems for printing on laser printers.
Print queue	A list of print jobs waiting to be sent to a printer.
Program	A set of instructions which cause a computer to perform tasks.

Protocol	A set of rules or standards that define how computers communicate with each other.
Query	The set of keywords and operators sent by a user to a search engine, or a database search request.
Queue	A list of e-mail messages waiting to be sent over the Internet.
RAM	Random Access Memory. The computer's volatile memory. Data held in it is lost when power is switched off.
Real mode	MS-DOS mode, typically used to run programs, such as MS-DOS games, that will not run under Windows.
Refresh	To update displayed information with current data.
Registered file type	File types that are tracked by the system registry and are recognised by the programs you have installed on your computer.
Registry	A database where information about a computer's configuration is deposited. The registry contains information that Windows continually references during its operation.
Remote computer	A computer that you can access only by using a communications line or a communications device, such as a network card or a modem.
Resource	A directory, or printer, that can be shared over a network.
Robot	A Web agent that visits sites, by requesting documents from them, for the purposes of indexing for search

	engines. Also known as Wanderers, Crawlers, or Spiders.
ROM	Read Only Memory. A PC's non-volatile memory. Data is written into this memory at manufacture and is not affected by power loss.
Root	The highest or uppermost level in a hierarchically organised disc directory.
Screen saver	A moving picture or pattern that appears on your screen when you have not used the mouse or keyboard for a specified period of time.
Script	A type of program consisting of a set of instructions to an application or tool program.
Scroll bar	A bar that appears at the right side or bottom edge of a window.
Search	Submit a query to a search engine.
Search engine	A program that helps users find information across the Internet.
Serial interface	An interface that transfers data as individual bits.
Server	A computer system that manages and delivers information for client computers.
Shared resource	Any device, program or file that is available to network users.
Shareware	Software that is available on public networks and bulletin boards. Users are expected to pay a nominal amount to the software developer.

Shortcut	A link to any item accessible on your computer or on a network, such as a program, file, folder, disc drive, Web page, printer, or another computer.
Signature file	An ASCII text file, maintained within e-mail programs, that contains text for your signature.
Site	A place on the Internet. Every Web page has a location where it resides which is called its site.
Software	The programs and instructions that control your PC.
Spamming	Sending the same message to a large number of mailing lists or newsgroups. Also to overload a Web page with excessive keywords in an attempt to get a better search ranking.
Spider	See robot.
Standby	A state in which your computer consumes less power when it is idle, but remains available for immediate use.
Subscribe	To become a member of.
Surfing	The process of looking around the Internet.
System files	Files used by Windows to load, configure, and run the operating system.
Task Manager	A utility that provides information about programs and processes running on the computer. Using Task Manager, you can end or run programs and end processes, and

	display a dynamic overview of your computer's performance.
Text file	An unformatted file of text characters saved in ASCII format.
Toggle	To turn an action on and off with the same switch.
Tool	Software program used to support Web site creation and management.
Toolbar	A bar containing icons giving quick access to commands.
TrueType fonts	Fonts that can be scaled to any size and print as they show on the screen.
Uninstall	When referring to software, the act of removing program files and folders from your hard disc and removing related data from your registry so the software is no longer available.
UNIX	Multitasking, multi-user computer operating system that is run by many computer servers on networks.
Upload/Download	The process of transferring files between computers. Files are uploaded from your computer to another and downloaded from another computer to your own.
URL	Uniform Resource Locator, the addressing system used on the Web, containing information about the method of access, the server to be accessed and the path of the file to be accessed.
USB	Universal Serial Bus - an external bus standard that enables data transfer rates of 12 Mbps.

Usenet	Informal network of computers that allow the posting and reading of messages in newsgroups that focus on specific topics.
User ID	The unique identifier, usually used in conjunction with a password, which identifies you on a computer.
Virtual Reality	Simulations of real or imaginary worlds, rendered on a flat two-dimensional screen but appearing three-dimensional.
Virus	A malicious program, downloaded from a web site or disc, designed to wipe out information on your computer.
Web	A network of hypertext-based multimedia information servers. Browsers are used to view any information on the Web.
Web Page	An HTML document that is accessible on the Web.
Wizard	A Microsoft tool that asks you questions and then creates an object depending on your answers.

Index

Companion Discs

COMPANION DISCS are available for some of the computer books written by the same author(s) and published by BERNARD BABANI (publishing) LTD, as listed at the front of this book (except for those marked with an asterisk).

There is no Companion Disc for this book

To obtain companion discs for other books, fill in the order form below, or a copy of it, enclose a cheque (payable to **P.R.M. Oliver**) or a postal order, and send it to the address given below. **Make sure you fill in your name and address** and specify the book number and title in your order.

Book No.	Book Name	Unit Price	Total Price
BP		£3.50	
BP		£3.50	
BP		£3.50	
Name		Sub-total	£.............
Address		P & P (@ 45p/disc)	£.............
		Total Due	£.............
Send to: P.R.M. Oliver, West Trevarth House, West Trevarth Nr Redruth, Cornwall, TR16 5TJ			

PLEASE NOTE

The author(s) are fully responsible for providing this Companion Disc service. The publishers of this book accept no responsibility for the supply, quality, or magnetic contents of the disc, or in respect of any damage, or injury that might be suffered or caused by its use.

Notes